WHAT PEOPLE ARE SAYING ABOUT KATHY DEGRAW AND *MIND BATTLES*...

My friend Kathy DeGraw has written a book that every believer needs to read. It doesn't matter whether you are a new believer or if you are a "seasoned saint"—this book is for you! As I've spent the past quarter century ministering in more than eighty nations around the world, I've discovered that the greatest battle everyone is facing, regardless of cultural background or social status, is the mind war. Yes, the mind is the location of your greatest spiritual warfare. Thankfully, Kathy has now written this powerful book that contains not only insight into our mind battles and how to overcome them, but also strategic activations that will help you to win this war *every time*! Through reading this book, I have personally gleaned some new revelation and received new tools that will be extremely useful to me in the days ahead. God desires for you to live a life of victory in His glory. He desires for you to win your *Mind Battles*.

—*Joshua Mills*
Best-selling author, *Moving in Glory Realms*

The devil bombards the mind with fear, worry, and panic! What if you could shield his attack and only think and then say good and pleasant thoughts? You will change *your* world and *the* world! *Mind Battles* is a "how to" book that is your difference maker!

—*Sid Israel Roth*
Host, *It's Supernatural*

T0051352

Mind Battles is an essential and important book for this hour that must be read carefully. Apostolic leader and spiritual warfare expert Kathy DeGraw has written another powerful warfare manual to arm the body of Christ. I have personally read and endorsed some of her most recent art of warfare books but this one by far is one of my favorites. She unpacks and unleashes sound biblical teachings, references, and real-life spiritual experiences and encounters to assist every reader on how to win the battlefield of the mind. *Mind Battles* exposes the enemy's insidious unseen tactics and attacks on the believer's mind to manipulate, influence, and trigger a cycle of defeat. This power-packed book will activate the shield of faith that every believer should take up so they are able to quench every fiery dart sent.

This excellent book is for now and for every leadership team, intercessor, cell group, spiritual warfare/deliverance worker, and saint who is ready to defeat the works of the devil. We must understand primarily that spiritual warfare consists of day-to-day battles against invisible evil forces that plague our minds. The Bible is clear that this is not a battle that is fought on a physical plane, but rather a spiritual one. *Mind Battles* is not just a book for just a few spiritual people but it's for *all* who are ready to wield their spiritual weapon of warfare to cast down imaginations and every high thing that exalts itself against the knowledge of God, bringing into captivity every thought to the obedience of Christ for victorious living. (See 2 Corinthians 10:4–5.) Must read! Must do!

—*Dr. Hakeem Collins*
Prophetic leader; international speaker
Senior leader, Glory Central Hub, Wilmington, DE
Author, *Unseen Warfare*

Mind Battles by Kathy DeGraw is an excellent resource/manual for gaining freedom and deliverance from spiritual attacks and bouts of depression as we learn how to deal with our own flaws as well as demonic attacks. Each chapter contains prophetic activations that I know you will find both useful and encouraging. The combination of biblical insight and practical activations will lead you to the kind of freedom and joy you have always wanted.

—Joan Hunter
Evangelist; host, *Miracles Happen* TV show

I started reading this book as an endorsement, but ended up identifying an area in my life where I needed freedom, and I found myself actually praying the prayers outlined in this book! I would highly recommend *Mind Battles* as a must-read.

—Apostle Alexander Pagani
Best-selling author, *The Secrets to Deliverance*

In Kathy DeGraw's latest literary endeavor, *Mind Battles*, she tackles a subject that will trigger a shaking in the kingdom of Satan—the mind. This is literally and spiritually where most demonic battles are won or lost. DeGraw presents efficacious strategies and secrets that will empower the believer against the machinations of the satanic realm. Her transparency here is refreshing. Kathy uses her own real-life experiences to augment the various topics she has written about. She totally exposes herself here and that's a great thing for the reader!

DeGraw has included prophetic activations, prayers, declarations, and a plan of action that can be used at any time by the reader. In my opinion, this book is packed with essential information and revelation regarding prophetic deliverance of the soul (mind, body, and emotions). I believe that this is one of Kathy's greatest literary works to date!

—John Veal
Author, *Supernaturally Delivered*
and *Supernaturally Prophetic*

Armed and loaded with powerful prophetic application and revelation, this book is a Titanic-sized blow to the enemy's camp! I am excited to hear of the many testimonies of people being set free from *Mind Battles* as the result of this on-time book for this season!

—Joel Yount
Encourager; author; speaker
Host, *The Joel Yount Program*

Mind Battles is a timely book that has been penned strategically by Kathy DeGraw. As an apostolic leader, she has given this and successive generations a tactical warfare manual. Kathy DeGraw is a warfare strategist with powerful prophetic insights demonstrated in her deliverance ministry. In this uniquely written book, she has taken us into one of the most choice battlegrounds of the enemy in spiritual warfare—*the mind*. As I read each chapter, Kathy almost literally takes the reader prophetically into the war room of the enemy like Elisha the prophet, who was able to expose the thoughts, the war strategies, and the plans of the enemy in his bedchambers. (See 2 Kings 6:12.)

I strongly endorse and recommend this book by my friend Kathy DeGraw, who has shared with us her expertise and experience as a treasure to learn and rediscover the art of war. *Mind Battles* will arm every believer in psychological warfare with unseen weaponry and scriptural fortitude to counterattack any and every demonic trigger and landmine set up against your destiny. This must-read epitomizes: *"For the weapons of our warfare are not carnal but mighty in God for pulling down strongholds, casting down arguments and every high thing that exalts itself against the knowledge of God, bringing every thought into captivity to the obedience of Christ"* (2 Corinthians 10:4–5 NKJV). I believe wholeheartedly that Kathy, in this well-written book, has revealed one of the powerful facets of the ministry of Jesus in bringing holistic healing, deliverance, and restoration in the mind.

—Dr. Naim Collins
League of the Prophets, Wilmington, DE
Author, *Realms of the Prophetic* and *Power Prophecy*

Outside of the Bible, *Mind Battles* is the best and most practical tool for overcoming struggles in your thought life that I have ever encountered. As one of the most profound and seasoned prophetic and deliverance voices today, Kathy DeGraw has created a tactical manual for exposing the works of darkness and winning the war in your mind. By applying the freedom applications, prophetic prayers, declarations, and activations that she provides, you will experience transformation in even the strongest negative thought patterns.

—*Mike Signorelli*
Senior pastor, V1 Church

MIND
BATTLES

MIND
BATTLES

ROOT OUT
MENTAL TRIGGERS TO
RELEASE PEACE

KATHY DeGRAW

WHITAKER
HOUSE

Note: This book is not intended to provide medical advice or to take the place of medical advice and treatment from your personal physician. Neither the publisher nor the author takes any responsibility for any possible consequences from any action taken by any person reading or following the information in this book. Always consult your physician or other qualified health care professional before undertaking any change in your physical regimen, whether fasting, diet, medications, or exercise.

Unless otherwise indicated, all Scripture quotations are taken from *The Holy Bible, Modern English Version.* Copyright © 2014 by Military Bible Association. Published and distributed by Charisma House. All rights reserved. Scripture quotations marked (NKJV) are taken from the *New King James Version,* © 1982 by Thomas Nelson, Inc. Used by permission. All rights reserved. Scripture quotations marked (CJB) are taken from *The Complete Jewish Bible,* © 1998 by David H. Stern. Published by Jewish New Testament Publications, Inc. Used by permission. All rights reserved.

Unless otherwise indicated, dictionary definitions are taken from *Merriam-Webster.com,* © 2022 Merriam-Webster, Inc.

MIND BATTLES
Root Out Mental Triggers to Release Peace

www.kathydegrawministries.org
www.facebook.com/kathydegraw
www.youtube.com/c/KathyDeGraw

ISBN: 978-1-64123-971-4
eBook ISBN: 978-1-64123-972-1

Printed in Colombia
© 2023 by Kathy DeGraw

Whitaker House
1030 Hunt Valley Circle
New Kensington, PA 15068
www.whitakerhouse.com

Library of Congress Cataloging-in-Publication Data (Pending)

1 2 3 4 5 6 7 8 9 10 11 ⅏ 30 29 28 27 26 25 24 23

DEDICATION

To Lauren:

You know all the reasons why I am dedicating this book to you. I couldn't have done it without all the brainstorms, freedom sessions, and discernment prayers. Thank you for your prophetic insights, life applications, and contributions to this book.

I love you!

CONTENTS

FOREWORD

During His time on earth, Jesus Christ was in the ministry of deliverance, often casting evil spirits out of people, freeing them from demonic possession and torment.

Following His crucifixion and resurrection, and just before His ascension into heaven, Jesus told His disciples, *"Go into all the world, and preach the gospel to every creature"* (Mark 16:15).

He told them, *"These signs will accompany those who believe: In My name they will cast out demons"* (verse 17).

In Luke 10:1–17, we read Jesus sent out seventy followers *"two by two"* into the places where He was about to go and minister. They later *"returned with joy, saying, 'Lord, even the demons are subject to us through Your name.'"*

Today, Satan, full of hatred for God and His people, *"knows that his time is short"* (Revelation 12:12), so he is waging an all-out war on humanity to deceive *"the whole world"* (Revelation 12:9), *"to steal and kill and destroy"* (John 10:10), and to drag as many as he can into hell with him.

In this war raging between the forces of the devil and his demons and the Lord and His angels, the primary battlefield is in our minds. Satan is a master military strategist skilled in the use of psychological warfare and deception. He knows that if he and his demons can control what we think, they can control us and misdirect the destiny God intended for our lives.

In today's increasingly chaotic world, many people are plagued by stress, fear, worry, anxiety, depression, confusion, anger, addictions, rejection, and feelings of condemnation. All these involve attacks on the mind, whether from ourselves, others, or thoughts that the enemy uses to oppress and deceive us.

In *Mind Battles*, my friend Kathy DeGraw helps you win the mind battles by revealing how the Holy Spirit can transform your life by guiding you in changing the way you think. Kathy is a prophetic deliverance minister who has given me and my wife Irene accurate prophetic words in the past. She is also a regular contributor to our news magazine *Prophecy Investigators*.

Based on what Kathy has learned from decades in ministry as well as wisdom and insights from Scripture, she shows how you can gain freedom from fear, stress, and torment, learning to how to bring *"every thought into captivity to the obedience of Christ"* (2 Corinthians 10:5) and set your mind *"on things above, not on things on earth"* (Colossians 3:2).

Mind Battles shows you how to take authority over your thoughts and circumstances in life, and how to be victorious with the help of the Holy Spirit by putting on *"the whole armor of God that you may be able to stand against the schemes of the devil"* (Ephesians 6:11).

Each chapter features "Warfare Prophetic Declarations" and "Prophetic Applications" that will help you successfully fight these spiritual battles and discover what is holding you back from the fullness God has planned for your life.

As you pray these "Warfare Prophetic Declarations" and do the exercises at the end of each chapter, you'll discover how to draw close to and partner with God, walking in the supernatural power, protection, and provision of the Holy Spirit.

Ever since meeting Kathy when I was executive editor of *Charisma* magazine and Charisma Media, my wife and I have often prayed the prophetic declarations that she sent us. Meanwhile, "The Log of Miracles and Supernatural Phenomena" that I began keeping in 2016 has grown to more than 170 pages with over 245 entries of miracle after miracle. I can only attribute this to the supernatural intervention of the Holy Spirit in our lives.

Instead of listening to the voice of the enemy, you'll discover in *Mind Battles* how the Holy Spirit speaks to our human spirits and our minds. When you are filled with the Holy Spirit, your discernment in the battlefield of the mind increases, and you're able to move prophetically, being led by the Spirit.

Throughout *Mind Battles*, Kathy DeGraw shares the trials, tragedies, and victories she's experienced in her life and ministry. She also shares the life-transforming realization that the biblical key to good relationships, health, finances, and becoming the person God intended you to be is centered on victory in the battlefield of the mind.

—*Troy Anderson*
Executive editor, *The Return International*

ACKNOWLEDGMENTS

It was my dream to publish this book. If I can set one person free, it will be time well spent. I've had an incredible support team who I'd like to thank for all their work in getting out the message the Lord has called me to share with the world.

Christine: The first time we spoke, there was an instant connection. I felt as if I was home and you said, "Welcome to the family." Thank you for believing the world needed to be set free of *Mind Battles* and that I could write this book on a short deadline.

David: You believed in me and made me the writer I am today. With every book, I push harder, and it becomes better because of you. Thank you for making *Mind Battles* possible. Words can't describe the gratitude in my heart. Thank you for your friendship and coaching.

Ron: My husband and friend, thank you for supporting me and believing I could write a book in thirty days! I did it!

Dillon, Amber, Josh, Lauren, and Alex: Thank you for your love, prayers, and all of your sacrifices over the years while I set the captives free.

Tracy: Thank you, my friend, for always grounding me, pushing me, getting me to see the bright side of things, being humble and honest, and listening to my successes and stressors. I love you, girlfriend!

Shiloh: For being my writing buddy and laying at my feet, in the sand, or sometimes with your pouty snout on my keyboard, for getting up and following me every time I needed to change to a new place to write. You are the best puppy in the world.

David M.: I wouldn't be where I am without you! Thank you for your friendship and believing in the big picture, constantly pushing me, giving me new ideas, the hours of work, phone calls, brainstorming, marketing, and everything else you do and have done for me. I could write an entire book in gratitude of your support for me.

Shawn A.: My friend, thank you for continually believing in me and the plan that God has for my life, for being one of my biggest cheerleaders, and for consistently putting up with my grammar and punctuation errors as you edit my articles.

My team, interns, and inner circle mentees: Thank you for your continued support and prayers!

Whitaker House team: Thank you to everyone who has made this such an enjoyable experience.

Peg: Thank you for taking my writing and making it sound like a symphony. I am completely in awe of what you've done and look forward to the writer I will become after I read and study how you made it flow so beautifully.

INTRODUCTION

Years ago, I lacked the necessary tools to destroy the devil's attacks on my mind. He targeted me relentlessly for far too long, leaving me feeling bound, emotionally paralyzed, and tormented.

Father God never wanted us to suffer from mind battles. He created us in His image to live on the mountaintop, not surrender to the enemy in dark valleys that leave us feeling helpless and hopeless.

My deepest desire for this book is that it will truly set the captives free. I long for you to obtain freedom in your mind, for this is where all battles begin and end. The mind truly is a battlefield. When we identify the battle, we can remove it. More than that, however, we must destroy it at its root.

It's important to recognize that *you* must fight for your freedom. You are the only one who can win the battle. I will give you the tools, but you need to apply them. This is not a book to read to pass the time and set aside once you're finished. Instead, I've written it as a manual for freedom, with several exercises and applications to release your mind from any thoughts that are tormenting you.

It brings me great joy to pay back the enemy of our souls for the years he kept me in bondage by helping others find their freedom too.

Father God gave you a destiny that you are to walk in, and every day you are in bondage, you aren't walking in the full potential which He created you to release. Jesus told us to *make disciples of all nations*" (Matthew 28:19). I take that charge seriously. I believe deliverance and discipleship go hand in hand, that you cannot have one without the other. You must not only receive deliverance but you need to learn how to keep your mind free.

Winning the battle of the mind is possible, but you have to fight when you don't feel like fighting. You have to speak with gratitude on your lips and in your heart when you feel like being negative. You can't allow defeat to penetrate your mind and whatever dark place you are in right now. You have to be so determined that you can win the battle that you are willing to do whatever it takes to persevere.

The battle is yours. It may have been planted from a trauma, a demonic attack, or a generational curse, but it's still *your* battle. If you've been looking for others to set you free, now is the time to use the keys that Jesus has given you to experience that liberation.

"*If the Son sets you free, you shall be free indeed*" (John 8:36). May you soon discover the freedom Jesus longs to give you as you read through these pages. Your life will never be the same.

OPENING PROPHETIC WORD

My opening instructions are that I am, Yes and Amen. I am your present help. I am there in that time of trouble and need. I will wash every tear away of mind-binding torment. I knitted you and formed you in your mother's womb. I knew what you were going to go through. I know the torment, the anxiety, the mental anguish, the fatigue, the worry, and the fear. I have seen it all. I know the bondage and the torment you have felt. I am here to be your healer, your Jehovah Rapha. I am here to be your deliverer. I purchased your deliverance at the cross. Now you and I together are going to walk out and manifest your deliverance, your freedom in your mind. I will give you tools as you partner with the Holy Spirit and allow Me to speak to you and guide you through your thinking. You will receive new discernment and revelation of how to conquer mind battles. It has been a long journey. It has been a tough journey. It has been a traumatizing journey. But you can be and you will be set free. Believe in yourself and believe in Me. I have penned these pages that you are about to read. I am the author and am giving you the tools. Now come on this journey to freedom with Me and trust Me to get free, stay free, and set others free in return.

1

MENTAL TRIGGERS WE ENCOUNTER

The mind is a battlefield, but it doesn't have to be. In my case, fearful thoughts tormented me for years. I am a worshipper who loves to spend time in God's presence, but there were times when torment and fear would attack my mind while I was trying to pray and worship. I'd fight to pull my thoughts in a positive direction, but the lure and pull of fear plagued me. I would feel emotionally paralyzed, unable to redirect my thoughts in a positive direction.

This battle of mine was the result of a generational curse and observations during my childhood. I saw people overreacting to certain situations with fear, and I learned to respond with fear. For instance, if a thunderstorm was predicted, they would panic and prepare for the worst possible outcomes, all the while speaking fearfully about what was approaching and what could happen. When a slight health ailment or simple affliction targeted someone in our family, pessimistic words were spoken about what could happen to that person, even when the issue was so minuscule that it didn't even merit a doctor's visit. When the fire sirens went off within minutes after a teenager left the house, someone would go check to make sure they were okay.

As a result, I had many mind obstacles, fear, and torment to overcome. I had to renew my mind and watch my words so I didn't put curses on my kids. When they left on snowy roads I had to say,

"Have fun; may angels guard and protect you," instead of, "Be careful—don't get in an accident." I had to overcome fear of storms, and eventually, so did my girls. Thankfully, we all overcame. We still don't like strong winds and some storms, but we are no longer fearful. There is a difference between not liking something and fearing it.

A GENERATIONAL CURSE OF FEAR

It took me years to overcome medical and health fears. It didn't help that I had unusual issues arise that contributed to the fear, but I believe it all began as a generational curse, which led to familiar spirits targeting attacks against my family. There were times I felt as if I was brainwashed to fear. To me, fear was a normal response to situations, and it was usually my first reaction. Later, I learned it wasn't the only reaction.

Eradicating stress, fear, rejection, and negativity from our thoughts can be difficult, but not impossible. God's Word tells us, "*With God all things are possible*" (Matthew 19:26).

My challenge was I didn't *know* I was in a battle. I had known fear for so long that I didn't think I could be free or how to gain that freedom. No one ever talked to me about what I was experiencing. Even as a Christian, I wasn't taught techniques to pull my mind back into good and godly thoughts. I lived with the torment until I learned of God's delivering power. His Word says, "*God has not given us the spirit of fear, but of power, and love, and self-control*" (2 Timothy 1:7), which also means self-discipline. I didn't know I could control my thoughts instead of my thoughts controlling me.

> EVEN AS A CHRISTIAN, I WASN'T TAUGHT HOW TO FIGHT NEGATIVE THOUGHTS SO I COULD PULL MY MIND BACK INTO GOOD AND GODLY THOUGHTS.

I needed tools. I needed instructions on how to pull my thoughts toward goodness and God. I needed to know the battle I was facing and how it manifested.

I could identify the mental triggers that would set me off and bring fear and torment. I knew thinking about certain things, such as sickness or money, would fill me with fear. So did experiencing some of life's challenges, such as driving on snowy or icy roads, being in a high place, or driving on a bridge over water. I knew fear would overwhelm me in certain situations or when I felt certain things, but I didn't realize I was in a dual battle—one of the flesh and one with principalities and powers. Therefore, I did only what I knew how to do and sought the Lord.

LYING PROSTRATE BEFORE THE LORD

Remember, I loved to worship. I ended up spending two years of my life prostrate on the floor with the greatest team of three: Father God, Jesus His Son, and the Holy Spirit. I didn't have to work and my kids were in school, so I could spend all day in the presence of the Lord. I went to church several times a week, studied the Word of God, read many books, prayed, worshipped, and pressed into Jesus as much as I could.

No one ever taught me to pray and fast. In fact, I didn't know about fasting because we had come out of a religious system that didn't teach it. I simply wanted all I could get of Jesus. I was with Him day and night. Sometimes I'd sleep in the presence of God on my living room floor. I didn't want to go to bed at night because I wanted to be with Him.

My kids knew that if I was on the floor, I was praying. They left me alone unless they needed me for something important. There were some nights that the presence of the Lord was so strong that I couldn't even get up to make dinner. I'd crawl across the floor, reach in my purse, grab a twenty-dollar bill, and ask my husband to order a pizza for himself and the kids.

God's Word filled my heart.

I will bless the LORD at all times; His praise will continually be in my mouth...I sought the LORD, and He answered me, and delivered me from all my fears.   (Psalm 34:1, 4)

Deliverance wasn't instant. I didn't get up off the floor with a supernatural mind transformation. However, I received revelation, deliverance, and some of the necessary tools to continue walking out my deliverance. The Bible says, *"Work out your own salvation"* (Philippians 2:12). *Merriam-Webster's Dictionary* defines *salvation* as "deliverance from the power and effects of sin." Your deliverance is a process you need to work out and walk out.

OUR MIND IS A BATTLEFIELD

We all have mind battles—things that trigger our thought processes to go into overdrive with worry, stress, anxiety, analysis paralysis, and fear. We can relate to these feelings because we've experienced one or more of them on multiple occasions throughout our lives. It's a struggle because these emotions are controlling us.

> WE ALL HAVE MIND BATTLES—THINGS THAT TRIGGER OUR THOUGHT PROCESSES TO GO INTO OVERDRIVE WITH WORRY, STRESS, ANXIETY, ANALYSIS PARALYSIS, AND FEAR.

We cannot win the battle until we understand it.

Our mind is so intricate that it can process a wide range of emotions and thoughts, from joy to sorrow, from our shopping list to world problems. We analyze, ponder, and overthink situations. Our mind runs rampant with vain imaginations and false scenarios. Our minds can think, visualize, and construct the words we want to say, create fantastic movie characters, costumes, and set designs, and so much more. I've often wondered how people think all this stuff up.

However, all the fascinating things the mind can do and the different directions it can go also explains why our mind can be a battlefield.

TWO SOURCES OF OUR THOUGHTS

Our thoughts come either from our own minds or an attack from the enemy. The latter is a lie that we believe, leading to spiritual warfare. No matter what the source, however, we can capture and control our thoughts.

Our thoughts are emotion-based reactions to life. We often entertain negativity. We'll think about an offense, guilt, rejection, or fear, and entertain it instead of dismissing it. Then it becomes part of us. As we focus on the negative, what didn't happen, or things that didn't go our way, we begin to spiral downward in our thinking. We focus on our circumstances instead of praying to turn our situation around or believing the Lord will manifest His best in our life. We start to feel bad about ourselves and what has happened, drawing us into depression, defeat, and fear.

We've all heard the lies of the enemy:

+ *You're no good.*

+ *You're never going to amount to anything.*

+ *No one will ever love you.*

+ *No one cares about you.*

+ *Why don't you kill yourself?*

When we hear negative words from our family, friends, coworkers, or others, the enemy is quick to use them to trigger negative thoughts such as these in our minds. We start to believe the lies, and they become us. The enemy has ensnared us in a mind battle.

Tormenting thoughts that the world would be better off without them can cause people to contemplate suicide. But it's all a lie! God put each one of us on this earth for a reason. Scripture tells us:

> *For I know the plans that I have for you, says the* LORD, *plans for peace and not for evil, to give you a future and a hope.*
> (Jeremiah 29:11)

> *For we are His workmanship, created in Christ Jesus for good works, which God prepared beforehand, so that we should walk in them.*
> (Ephesians 2:10)

Don't allow the devil to steal your destiny. Don't harm yourself and hurt those who love you through your demise. Your life is worth living. How do I know that? Because right now, I am hearing the Holy Spirit prophetically speak to me. He is telling me to put this part about suicide and wanting to kill yourself in this book. He wants to save your life and tell you that you are worth everything. Your life is worth living. God has a mission and a purpose for you, a kingdom assignment for you to accomplish. There is a portion of the world that you need to change and reach for Jesus Christ. He has plans and ways that are higher than your ways. (See Isaiah 55:8–9.)

GOD HAS A MISSION AND A PURPOSE FOR YOU.
THERE IS A PORTION OF THE WORLD THAT YOU NEED TO CHANGE
AND REACH FOR JESUS CHRIST.

The devil is *"the father of lies"* (John 8:44), who has only come to *"steal and kill and destroy"* (John 10:10). He tries to take away everything good, including God's plans for us, but Jesus came so that we may have life and *"have it more abundantly."*

Every minute you are not abundantly living, you are dying emotionally, which attacks your body physically.

FREEDOM APPLICATION

As I write this, I feel that the Holy Spirit wants to come in and deliver someone—likely many people—as you read this next part. I feel Him releasing the ministry of deliverance. Raise your expectations. Right now, the Holy Spirit is delivering you from some mind captivity. Yes, you will need to walk out some of your freedom and change thought patterns. I know the Holy Spirit is speaking to someone. He is ministering to your heart. He is delivering you from captivity in your mind. He loves you that much; He wants to intervene supernaturally on your behalf as you simply read this book, open your heart to the message being presented, and surrender your mind, will, and emotions to what He wants to do in your life. You are worth it all. You are worth everything to Him. Press in and press through to your breakthrough.

PROPHETIC PRAYER

Make a conscious decision today. Say and speak audibly:

This is my time. This is my moment. This is my season of divine breakthrough. This is the moment I turn around. I'm not going back. I'm moving forward. I'm no longer going to allow torment in my mind. I am no longer going to be depressed. Depression, I command you to leave. I speak and declare that the joy of the Lord is my strength. I don't have to do life alone. I have a Helper, the Holy Spirit, to lead and guide me through my day. Jesus loves me and died for me, which is more than enough. I will not allow torment, rejection, depression, stress, anxiety, unworthiness, and fear to control me anymore. I take back my thoughts. I take a prophetic action. I command a spiritual shift and emotional renewal to come forth. I press forward and am not looking back. I have hope! I have joy! I live life abundantly! I am satisfied with the goodness of the Lord upon me at all times! I pray, speak, and command these things to come forth into total manifestation, in Jesus's name! Amen!

FREEDOM APPLICATION

I feel a deliverance anointing right now. I believe the Lord is doing amazing work in your life. Believe and receive the liberation He wants to give you. I want to pray for you right now.

Father God, in the name of Yeshua Messiah, I lift up my friends who are reading this right now. I speak and decree the shalom peace of God to come upon them right now. I speak for peace to come forth where torment has been. Give them the peace that surpasses all understanding. I thank You, Lord, that You love my friends and readers, and right now, I ask for them to feel the tangible presence of that love. Fill them up with fresh hope, joy everlasting, and the peace that only comes from You. I command and call forth peace to come, and negativity, stress, and anxiety to leave. Where they feel hopeless, Lord, give them hope. Put people in their path to support them and help them receive the freedom they so desperately long for, in Jesus's name. Amen!

WHAT TRIGGERS YOUR BATTLE

Discovering the trigger to your mind battle will expose the enemy and make you consciously aware of your thoughts when they head in an unproductive and unfruitful direction. Be alert to your triggers. Write them down or make a mental note, so you know when to remove yourself from the situation, change a conversation, or move in another direction. Recognize where the enemy attacks and what makes your mind work overtime with vain imaginations and false scenarios.

> DISCOVERING THE TRIGGER TO YOUR MIND BATTLE WILL MAKE YOU CONSCIOUSLY AWARE OF YOUR THOUGHTS WHEN THEY HEAD IN AN UNPRODUCTIVE AND UNFRUITFUL DIRECTION.

The emotional trigger that sets off your mind battle is unique to you. It could be a sin, trauma, emotional ailment, or an area where you need deliverance from strongholds. Every situation is different.

There's no cookie-cutter solution when it comes to deliverance or healing ministry. What works for one person may not work for another. In this book, I explain a variety of triggers to help you reach mental and emotional freedom. I come beside you to help you work it out and walk it out.

Here is a list of some triggers so you can get started right now.

RECOGNIZE SIN

One of the ways to determine your battle is to recognize the sin that is infiltrating your life and instigating a battle in your mind. For example, when you look at pornography, there is a lure into the sin of lust. The enemy whispers in your mind, "No one will know. Just look at that site on the Internet one more time," or, "It's okay. Everyone is doing it." The thoughts in your flesh justify your unclean actions, and the lies you believe intensify the battle that's holding you in bondage.

A food addiction may be rooted in an emotional ailment, such as a need for comfort, a feeling of loneliness, a desire for control, or an escape from boredom.

We can discover the battle when we recognize the sin in the first place. This opens doors and pathways to our hearts and minds. When we lie, cheat, steal, or have an addiction, we need to find the initial gateway and the lie that's compelling us to repeatedly sin.

All sin and open doorways have root causes and triggers that keep our mind stuck in the same negative patterns and habits. Once we discover the root cause or entry point, we can break the cycle. In my book *Unshackled*,[1] I explain how to discover and break free from the top ten strongholds in life.

DRAW OUT WORRY AND FEAR

Know where the enemy or your vain imaginations attack. Face your fear. If you are avoiding a person, place, or thing because of a past trauma, concern, or difficulty, you are attempting to mask the fear, not root it out.

> IF YOU ARE AVOIDING A PERSON, PLACE, OR THING
> BECAUSE OF A PAST TRAUMA, CONCERN, OR DIFFICULTY,
> YOU ARE ATTEMPTING TO MASK THE FEAR, NOT ROOT IT OUT.

I once ministered to a lady whose family owned a boat. They loved to cruise on a lake and took a special trip every year centered around the water. But this woman would abstain from certain water activities. After we became friends, I was invited on a trip, and she told me about her fear of water. She had been concealing her fear rather than facing it. I had a deliverance session with her, found the root cause of her trauma, and she was set free. She even bought a bathing suit for the vacation we took together.

1. Kathy DeGraw, *Unshackled: Breaking the Strongholds of Your Past to Receive Complete Deliverance* (Bloomington, MN: Chosen Books, 2020).

We need to root out our fears and destroy the effect they have on us.

I used to be hypersensitive to every abnormal noise my vehicle made. I was convinced that I going to break down while traveling with the kids or get into an accident. Every time I heard a creak, rattle, or some other weird noise, I would tell my husband when I returned home, "Honey, something is wrong with the van." This happened so often that he began to ignore me because he knew it was fear talking. When I finally got over it and something really *was* wrong with my vehicle, I had to persist and persuade him to check into it.

The enemy used my fear of vehicle problems to attack me. I knew it was the enemy because I could feel fear arise from within me. It wasn't a normal reactionary fear; it was as if something was piercing me and gripping me internally. It would honestly freak me out. When I discovered nothing wrong with my vehicle and realized it was the enemy attacking me, or vain imaginations or false scenarios playing out in my mind, I was able to begin to conquer my thoughts, rebuke the attacks, and take authority over them. Discerning and destroying the enemy's works and exposing the target of fear was instrumental in my life.

One time while I was on a ministry tour, the Spirit of the Lord told me that my car would break down three times before I returned. During the trip, the temperature gauge kept going in the red. Three times, we stopped at a vehicle repair shop. Finally, at the last stop, the mechanic took me over to look at all the gauges hooked up to the machine.

"Ma'am, there is nothing wrong," he said.

I knew then that I had been under a spiritual warfare attack. It was a confirmation of the word the Lord gave me in advance. Upon renewing my mind, the attacks ceased against future travels. The enemy was exposed and lost his foothold in my life. I now knew how to capture my thoughts and take authority over situations. I was free!

ROOTING OUT REJECTION

Many people suffer from the mind battle of rejection, which is commonly based on a lie. When you suffer from rejection, you hear lies in your mind that people are talking about you, that a friend likes someone else better, or that your boss is going to fire you. I remember a man who had such a fear of rejection that for years, he went into work daily believing he was going to get fired. He had to remove the lie, seek deliverance, and release rejection from his life.

When we root out the lie of rejection, we can step onto the pathway to freedom.

Rejection co-labors with the need for acceptance and people-pleasing. When we know a lie is triggering our thoughts, we can capture them and dismiss it, but we also have to work out an unhealthy need for acceptance and stop being doormats. This is where prophetic action and self-responsibility come into play. We need to recognize and remove the lie, which is a spiritual condition and emotional belief, but we also need to walk out behavior patterns, negative thoughts, and habits that cause us to crave validation.

A proper balance must occur between the reality that spiritual warfare occurs and the responsibility we have to control and manage our soul—our mind, will, and emotions. Not every battle can be blamed on a demon or spiritual warfare; many of the struggles we face and experience are of human origin.

NOT EVERY BATTLE CAN BE BLAMED ON A DEMON OR SPIRITUAL WARFARE; MANY OF THE STRUGGLES WE FACE AND EXPERIENCE ARE OF HUMAN ORIGIN.

One reason for the mind battles we face is that we haven't been taught to take authority over our thoughts. We get people to help us talk things out or process our emotions, but this does not provide practical tools to win the battle or discover and control mental triggers. We aren't learning to bring *"every thought into captivity to the obedience of Christ"* (2 Corinthians 10:5). If we don't capture our thoughts, they become us, but if we get to the root of our mental trigger, we can heal emotionally and spiritually.

Visual exercises can help us achieve freedom from a mind battle. The exercise here is designed to enable you to chart your triggers. In the circles around the central "ME" circle, write your feelings, such as rejection, anger, fear, worry, or depression. On the lines beside these smaller circles, note the things that trigger these feelings, such as feeling unloved, hurtful words, social media, coworkers, etc. Discovering what triggers your negative emotions can help you take steps to prevent them.

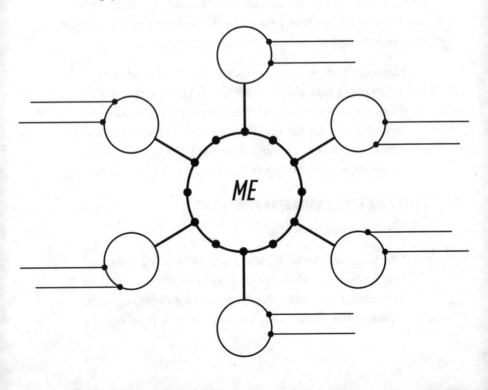

PROPHETIC ACTIVATION

IDENTIFY THE BATTLE

What is your battle? What consumes your thoughts? Ask yourself, "What are the main three things that hold me back from the fullness of God and walking in my destiny?" Your answers will assist you in identifying your battle.

Can you discern the root cause or entry point of these three things? The root cause is the event or situation that triggered the problem, while the entry point is the time period when the problem began. There could have been a number of things happening in your life around that time that impact the warfare you now experience.

FORGIVE AND REPENT

Once you have identified the battle, forgive anyone who was involved. Repent for any actions you took or unhealthy feelings you had toward another person. Speak audibly that you forgive these people, repent, and ask Jesus to forgive you:

> Heavenly Father, I forgive [*insert name(s)*] for what they did to me or how they made me feel. I choose this day to forgive them and release this hurt from my life. I ask Your forgiveness, Jesus, for any sin I committed or wrong mindsets I established. I receive Your forgiveness and release myself from the situation in Jesus's name. Amen.

TARGET THE BATTLE AND BREAK AGREEMENT

Speak out and decree:

> I break agreement with [*your issue*], and sin, rejection, and fear. I speak and declare that I will not allow my past to define me. I command the battle to cease in Jesus's name. I declare the victory that has been won. I proclaim the

battle no longer rages. I speak and decree that I have the victory. I pray and declare this prophetic prayer proclamation, in Jesus's name.

RELEASE DELIVERANCE

Jesus was in the ministry of deliverance and cast out evil spirits. You are walking out your mind bondage now. One of the keys to getting free and staying free is to cast out the correlating spirit that could be manifesting. Pray audibly and command the evil spirit to leave. It could be a spirit of lying, depression, worry, stress, anxiety, fear, mind-binding, or torment. Declare aloud, "Spirit of _____, I cast you out, in Jesus's name."

WARFARE PRAYER DECLARATIONS

+ I bind and restrict demonic attacks from coming against my mind in Jesus's name.

+ I proclaim every obstacle to gaining freedom in my mind is removed in Jesus's name.

+ I renounce negative thoughts that hold me in the wrong ways of thinking.

+ I rebuke and take authority over every thought of rejection. I decree I am accepted!

+ I live by the Word of God and capture every thought and subject it to the Word of God.

REMOVE THE BATTLE

How can you aim to think and react differently? Pray and seek the Holy Spirit. By thinking and partnering with the Holy Spirit, discern what is obtainable to you. This is an individual time for you to take a step of action and decide what will work best for you. You may have tried different things in the past, but you now know a little more about mind battles. Walk out, remove the battle, and receive freedom!

PROPHETIC APPLICATION

1. This chapter included a prayer that was a declaration and statement of faith. Spend time thinking about that prayer. What do you need that you currently lack? Write some additional sentences and prayer declarations to renew your mind.

2. While we want to lean on the Holy Spirit, a mentor can also help to keep us accountable as we walk out our freedom. Pray and discern if someone in your life can mentor you through this season. Ask the Holy Spirit to confirm it to you and that person. Approach the person and ask them if they would mentor you through your season of liberation from mind battles and hold you accountable to obtain and receive freedom.

FREEDOM THOUGHT

You were made in the image of God. (See Genesis 1:26–27.) No matter how troubled you are, your mind can be restored to that original image in which God created it.

2

IDENTIFY SOURCES OF MIND INFLUENCERS

When I was in elementary school, I disliked creative writing. Using my imagination to compose a story was uncomfortable and unfamiliar, and it stretched my thinking. Although I loved to read books and even participated in Book Bowl competitions, I didn't enjoy writing stories. I didn't have a creative imagination, nor did I know how to make up stories that flowed and sounded intriguing.

I rebelled against my language arts teachers. My skills in grammar and punctuation were abysmal. I mastered spelling somehow, making it to the final rounds of spelling bee competitions, but I still struggle with the rules of grammar and punctuation to this day. Praise the Lord for amazing editors!

When the Lord called me to be a writer, I kicked and screamed. My first two books were self-published purely out of obedience to Him. It wasn't until I allowed the Holy Spirit to take over my fingers to serve as His instrument, typing His words, that I began to enjoy the process. Now, I find writing therapeutic. I love intertwining life application, testimonies, and scriptural revelation to bring impartation to my readers. As a child, I didn't think I was creative, but creativity was in me all along because God designed us that way. We think and we create.

Thousands of thoughts fill our minds every day, and many of them involve our imagination. Where do all of those thoughts come from? How do thoughts of what might be infiltrate our minds? We will begin to answer these questions as we discover the mind influencers in our lives.

Discernment is the number one prayer request in my ministry. I wrote a book on discernment because people want to know, "How do I know the source of what I am hearing? Am I hearing from my own soul, demonic spirits from the enemy, or God?"

> MANY PEOPLE ARE SEEKING PRAYER FOR DISCERNMENT.
> THEY WANT TO DETERMINE WHETHER THEY ARE HEARING FROM THEIR
> OWN SOULS, DEMONIC SPIRITS, OR GOD.

When desiring discernment, it's important to recognize the voice of the deceiver, hear the voice of the Lord, and know how to identify our own thoughts.

Identifying the source of mind influencers in our lives is equally important. As we experience mind battles, knowing the basics of the struggle will assist us in evicting wrong thoughts and replacing them with the truth. One of the ways we identify the battle in which we attempt to gain liberation is to know what seed was planted there and by whom or what.

THREE SOURCES OF BATTLE

When the military engages in a war, they study their opponent. They want to discover how strong the enemy is, what type of weapons they have, and their known combat tactics.

Our first step in overcoming a mind battle is identifying our enemy and understanding their strengths and weaknesses. Whether we are dealing with vain imaginations, hurtful words spoken by another, or lies we believe, identifying the source of those thoughts can bring us victory on the battlefield.

Our battle comes from three different sources:

1. People: outside influencers, friends, family, and relationships
2. Evil spirits: demonic attacks and spiritual warfare
3. Ourselves: our soul, meaning our mind, will, and emotions (see chapter ten)

PEOPLE

People can contribute to our mind battles based on how we are treated and the words spoken to us or about us. They can make us feel victimized, offended, hurt, rejected, or betrayed. The adage "hurting people hurt people" is true. One of the reasons I desire healing for *you* is to prevent you from hurting others.

Mind bondage can come through hurtful words and situations. We cycle those conversations and events repeatedly in our minds. I refer it to as "sitting and thinking, rotting and stinking" because that is what we do. Replaying past hurts in our mind never leads to anything beneficial. It only causes further stress and anxiety about the situation.

You are guaranteed to get hurt. Jesus says, *"In the world you will have tribulation"* (John 16:33). It's what you do in those moments that matters. Choose peace. Choose to let the trouble roll off of you. Don't take it in. Don't allow it to enter your mind or heart. Envision it rolling off your shoulders, down to your hands and fingertips, and dropping off of you.

This is a choice I began to make years ago. I discovered that stress, anxiety, worry, and fear led to sickness and disease. Stress raises cortisol levels, which releases glucose into the bloodstream and can lead to Type 2 diabetes. A medical doctor once told me that stress can raise your blood glucose level "considerably." Through natural, emotional, and spiritual changes, I have helped people lower theirs, and doctors have verified the results.

An elevated cortisol level can lead to weight gain, hypertension, and insulin resistance; it can also affect the immune system, suppress digestion, and attack the reproductive system. Long-term stress and high cortisol levels can cause higher cholesterol and blood pressure levels as well as Type 2 diabetes, all contributors to heart disease.

Years ago, I decided not to allow rejection and offense to take hold of my mind or my heart. Stress, anxiety, and fear come from soul wounds of being rejected and offended. I love everyone reading this book and everyone I get to minister to. God has a plan for me to reach more people. If I allow ill emotions to take hold, I leave a door open to sickness and disease. That would inhibit me from completing my calling and being able to minister to all the wonderful people in the world whom God has called me to reach. Besides that, I am a wife, mother, and grandmother. I would hate to have my family lose me because of something I could have prevented by changing my reaction and attitude toward emotional responses to external circumstances.

> WHEN WE HAVE NEVER WORRIED BEFORE ABOUT SICKNESS OR FINANCES, AND A FRIEND STARTS TALKING TO US ABOUT THEIR OWN FEAR, OUR MINDS CAN RUN WILD.

It doesn't take much to realize that people influence our thinking. Take a look around. We are influenced by styles, media, health, and finances. People encourage us to give financially to a particular cause or have one bite of something we shouldn't when we're dieting—and we do it. When we have never worried before about sickness or finances, and a friend starts talking to us about their own fear, our minds can run wild, take hold of what that person said, and open the door to stress and anxiety. We may have felt unshakable, but being surrounded by people reacting to world news can affect us. We must be unmovable. We must learn to control our emotions.

The Bible warns us that what is in our hearts will manifest through us.

For as he thinks in his heart, so is he.   (Proverbs 23:7)

*A good man out of the good treasure of his heart bears what
is good, and an evil man out of the evil treasure of his heart
bears what is evil. For of the abundance of the heart his mouth
speaks.*   (Luke 6:45)

My emotional healing prevents other people from influencing
my thinking. I am unmovable. Others can't reject me or offend me.
I refuse to allow these emotions to cause sickness to attack my
body. My mouth is a vessel for the Holy Spirit. If I want good
to come out of my mouth, I need to check my mind and heart.
I cannot be offended or rejected because I am free from myself.
I know who I am in Christ. I don't seek anyone to validate me. I
know who I am. My identity is in Him! I have no need for affirma-
tion from people because my acceptance is in the Father.

EVIL SPIRITS

Evil spirits can attack you and send forth demonic assignments against your life. Monitoring spirits are familiar with how
you respond to stress, anxiety, fear, and worry. When you speak
stressful words audibly as you think negatively, demons are ready
to activate what you say. They are familiar with your seasons of
emotional turmoil and the demonic spiritual warfare attacks you
suffer. It is one of the reasons you can struggle and feel attacked
in the same areas and don't receive the freedom you desire. (See
chapter three for more on this matter.)

Evil spirits are fallen angels (see Revelation 12:7–9) that are
sent here to destroy. One of the ways they do this is through the
battle in your mind. The Bible warns us that the enemy comes to
disrupt our lives. Jesus says:

*The thief does not come, except to steal and kill and destroy. I
came that they may have life, and that they may have it more
abundantly.*   (John 10:10)

Every day that we are not abundantly living, a part of us is
emotionally dying. I like how *The Complete Jewish Bible* puts it:

"The thief comes only in order to steal, kill and destroy; I have come so that they may have life, life in its fullest measure" (CJB). As we struggle with mind battles, we aren't living the life Jesus came to give us in the fullest measure.

God never intended us to have mind battles. We are meant to have *"the mind of Christ"* (1 Corinthians 2:16). We cannot say, "I've always been this way," or "I'm never going to be set free." We cannot believe this is our fate when the Word of God gives us positive affirmations about the kind of life we are intended to live.

> WE CANNOT BELIEVE A MIND BATTLE IS OUR FATE
> WHEN GOD'S WORD GIVES US POSITIVE AFFIRMATIONS ABOUT THE
> KIND OF LIFE WE ARE INTENDED TO LIVE.

Demonic Influence

Evil spirits are sent on assignment *"to steal and kill and destroy"* (John 10:10). In Mark 5:1–20, we learn about a demon-possessed man who was terrorized in his mind. He had an unclean spirit, and he was violent, crying out and cutting himself with stones. A legion of demonic spirits had been oppressing the man, making him crazy and full of rage. After Jesus cast out the many demons, the man became in his right mind. He is found in verse 15 now clothed and sitting with Jesus.

How many actions or thoughts do we suffer from that could be demonically influenced? Could we be oppressed in our soul, with a demon causing us to think wrong thoughts so that we become filled with fear? Yes, we can!

I was bound in fear for forty years, even though I was a tongue-talking, Spirit-filled Christian who ministered all around the United States, casting out demons in thousands of deliverance sessions. All the while, I was bound to fear in certain areas of my life. It was not only fear but a demon of fear, and I could feel it manifest. I share this with you so you understand that if a deliverance minister like me could have a spirit of fear, so could you. If your problem is demonically influenced, seek the Holy Spirit to reveal or convict you.

> *Stay sober, stay alert! Your enemy, the Adversary, stalks about like a roaring lion looking for someone to devour.*
>
> (1 Peter 5:8 cjb)

The devil is seeking someone who is weak-minded, prayerless, and feeling victimized. I once heard a pastor say, "He can't devour everyone. He is seeking whom he may devour." The devil stakes out his prey. He's not as fast, smart, and powerful as we may think. Let's devour him with the power of our words before he devours us. Let's be proactive instead of reactive and pray on the offense rather than just on the defense. We must press through to our breakthrough at all times.

THE DEVIL IS SEEKING SOMEONE WHO IS WEAK-MINDED, PRAYERLESS, AND FEELING VICTIMIZED. LET'S DEVOUR HIM WITH THE POWER OF OUR WORDS BEFORE HE DEVOURS US.

Here's another visual exercise to help you determine what is influencing your thoughts. In this exercise, think about common words or phrases that you have and jot down where you think they are coming from. Decide whether you are hearing from your soul (your mind, will, or emotions); if God is speaking to you; or if the enemy is telling you lies.

Your Soul	God	The Enemy

OURSELVES

The third possible source of our mind battle is our own self. Our mind battle can be self-inflicted due to who we are, the worry we allow ourselves to feel, and the way we think. Understanding how our mind operates will assist us as we try to unpack our thoughts. The goal is to be able to create behavior patterns to manifest change.

In general, there are two ways in which our minds operate: through processing or analyzing.

Processors

Processors think through the information they have to figure out what happened and the end result or net effects of a particular incident. They break it down to help them process the information. They can't receive things at face value but need to discover what the circumstances mean in order to move forward.

While I was attending a conference with one of my assistants, there were unusual spiritual manifestations that we hadn't previously witnessed. Being analytical and a deliverance minister, I proceeded to minister to people and didn't give the manifestations a second thought. However, my assistant was a processor and as we walked back to our room, she said, "I have to process that out." She did not comprehend the unfamiliar situation, so she had to process her experience.

Analyzers

People who analyze consider the future and the outcome of a situation. They discern questions in their minds, such as, "How do I fix this?"

Business people and ministry leaders are often analyzers who may also operate in discernment. Analyzers seldom shut their brains down; they are always thinking about the next move. While processors want to figure things out, analyzers want to know why something happened and the outcome.

I used to analyze everything. I could be in worship with my hands raised high, focusing on Jesus—or so I thought—while I was analyzing at the same time.

I am very good at being consciously aware of every activity that is going on around me simultaneously. I do this so well that I can become hyper-analytical. While I believe being analytical is a gift, when we become hyper-analytical, we take a gift God has given us and misuse it to the point that it becomes a hindrance instead of a help.

If you too analyze everything and anything in sight, rest assured, you can change, just as I did. I now use discernment when thinking about a situation. I still analyze, but I no longer have to analyze during worship and have it distract me. I can focus on worshipping the Father *"in spirit and truth"* (John 4:23). I love to worship. If you saw me worship, you would see that, and might find it hard to imagine I ever started analyzing while I worshipped.

SPIRITUAL DISCERNMENT

Spiritual discernment is a gift from God, and it is one of the positive influencers on our minds. Discernment is how the Holy Spirit speaks to our human spirits and our minds. The Holy Spirit resides inside of us and communicates with us as we make Jesus the Lord and Savior of our lives. When we are filled with the Holy Spirit, we will increase in discernment and be able to move prophetically, being led by Him. As we are filled with the fire of God, the Spirit of the Lord will rest on us, bringing wisdom, understanding, counsel, might, knowledge, and reverence for God. (See Isaiah 11:2.) Discernment led by the Holy Spirit will assist us in gaining knowledge of the battle we are facing. Being in the secret place, the Spirit will speak to us about how to receive freedom in our minds.

I invite you to pray, "Holy Spirit, *'Create in me a clean heart'*" (Psalm 51:10). Earnestly pray, *"Search me, O God, and know my heart; try me, and know my concerns"* (Psalm 139:23).

WHEN WE ARE FILLED WITH THE HOLY SPIRIT,
WE WILL INCREASE IN DISCERNMENT AND BE ABLE TO MOVE
PROPHETICALLY, BEING LED BY HIM.

Invitation leads to conviction. The Holy Spirit will correct us. We will receive discernment in our situation. He will give us strategies with which to set ourselves free. John 16:8 says the Holy Spirit *"will convict the world of sin and of righteousness and of judgment."* What I say is, "Holy Spirit, peel me layer by layer like an onion, so there is nothing left but You."

When you learn the names of the Holy Spirit and His characteristics, you will discover His attributes, which can assist you in discerning what is from Him.[2]

IMAGINATION

Imagination is the creative ability of a thinking, active mind. Our minds are very inventive and ingenious. I am not a big movie fan, but I watch *Star Wars* movies with my husband Ron. I am always amazed at the creativity of the producers and writers to come up with movie ideas and then convey what they are seeking to the character designers, who then lay out the characters' overall visual appearance. I think these people must have very wild and creative imaginations.

Imagination is defined as "the act or power of forming a mental image of something not present to the senses or never before wholly perceived in reality." When He created us, Father God gave us minds that are capable of imagination.

And He has filled him with the Spirit of God, in wisdom, in understanding, and in knowledge, and in all manner of craftsmanship, to design artistic works.　　(Exodus 35:31–32)

2. The booklet *Life in the Spirit: In His Presence* includes a thirty-day devotional that I wrote on the different names and characteristics of the Holy Spirit. It's available at www.kathydegrawministries.org/product/life-in-the-spirit-in-his-presence.

For we are His workmanship, created in Christ Jesus for good
works, which God prepared beforehand, so that we should
walk in them.   (Ephesians 2:10)

When something negative happens in our lives, worry and
stress attack our minds, and we begin to play out worst-case scenarios in our heads.

If your boss comes to you Friday at 8 a.m. and says, "I need to
talk to you before you leave today," your mind might immediately
jump to the idea that you're going to be fired. You start to think
about what you could have done wrong, imagine how the conversation will go, and start crafting words to defend yourself. We rarely
think that our boss has something good to talk about.

The majority of our thoughts could be captured and dismissed
instead of entertained negatively if we would reel in what is out
of control. We have the power within us. We can ask the Holy
Spirit how to use the creativity in our minds to generate positive
thoughts and thus receive abundant peace.

PROPHETIC ACTIVATION

IDENTIFY THE BATTLE

Trust the Holy Spirit for any relationship He removes and
trust that He will give you some faith-filled friends. Pray, "Holy
Spirit, remove everything unproductive and unfruitful from my
life." I love the story of the paralytic in Mark 2:1–12. This man's
friends believed so strongly in Jesus that when they could not bring
their paralyzed friend into the house where He was preaching,
they opened up the roof and brought him in that way. We need
people like these in our lives, people who will build us up, stand
with us, and help us conquer the battle and not be part of it.

FORGIVE AND REPENT

Take a moment to write a list of people who have contributed
to your battle and bring the list before the Lord. Forgive them

just as Christ forgave you and asks you to do the same. (See, for example, Matthew 18:21–22; Luke 6:37.) Choose today to release forgiveness from relational hurts. Ask the Holy Spirit to convict you of areas where you had unhealthy emotions or reactions that contributed to the battle you experienced.

Pray aloud this prayer of forgiveness:

Holy Spirit, I ask You to partner with me right now. I want the enemy exposed. I want unclean and unhealthy emotions to leave me. This day, I choose peace, forgiveness, and love. Help me daily to live in assurance, knowing You are with me. When I feel heavy and burdened, help me to turn that stinking thinking into righteous living. I depend upon You to be my healer. I believe the heavenly Father is my justifier. I trust You and the wisdom of Your plan to remove everything and everyone from my life that is unproductive and unfruitful. I pray this in Jesus's name. Amen.

TARGET THE BATTLE AND BREAK AGREEMENT

Pronounce and declare:

I break agreement with vain imaginations, false scenarios, and useless thinking. I proclaim I will not allow what others speak about me or how they treat me to define me and cause my emotions to spiral downward. I am God's child. Jesus is my friend. The Holy Spirit is my helper. I have the greatest team of three—Father God, Jesus His Son, and the Holy Spirit—to think about and help me through difficult situations. I will rely on the Lord's love for me to get me through every battle. This is my confession of which I will take possession, in Jesus's name.

RELEASE DELIVERANCE

Jesus was in the ministry of deliverance and cast out evil spirits. As you walk out your mind bondage, one of the keys to getting free and staying free is to cast out the correlating spirit that could be manifesting. It may be a spirit of lying, depression, worry, stress, anxiety, fear, mind-binding, or torment. Pray audibly and command the spirit to leave. Say, "Spirit of _____, I cast you out, in Jesus's name."

WARFARE PRAYER DECLARATIONS

+ I break down mind bondage due to negative thinking. I will stop allowing negative thoughts.

+ I nullify every codependent action and emotion that leaves me in unhealthy relationships.

+ I uproot and remove completely every detouring thought that has weighed me down.

+ I rebuke and take authority over the enemy and every evil thought he sends my way.

+ I expel and force out every evil spirit penetrating my mind and causing destruction.

REMOVE THE BATTLE

The Holy Spirit told me years ago, "Kathy, you don't have to participate in anything that is a time waster and destiny stealer."

When so-called friends try to influence your thinking and engage you in negative or fearful conversations, how can you change the topic or choose not to participate? How can you guard your heart and mind?

PROPHETIC APPLICATION

1. You can train your mind to think creatively for the kingdom of God instead of allowing vain imaginations,

stress, and worry to infiltrate. Instead of imagining distressing scenarios and outcomes to relational situations, partner with the Holy Spirit to create something beautiful out of your thought life.

2. You need community, companionship, and relationships with family, friends, coworkers, neighbors, and fellow believers. But do you depend on them more than you depend on the Lord? Shift your focus and spend more time with Him. As you build a solid relationship with the Lord, you will still need people, but you will be less dependent on them. Then you will experience less hurt when someone lets you down.

FREEDOM THOUGHT

You aren't responsible for another person's actions. Release yourself from false responsibility and disappointment for others' behaviors, words, and actions.

3

BE AWARE OF THE SPIRITUAL BATTLE

Everything in my life would be propelling along just fine when I would suddenly be under intense spiritual warfare. I noticed the same cycles of struggle during specific times of the year. I began to detect relational attacks that occurred yearly in a particular month, bringing me to the point of deep turmoil. There were subtle differences in these events, but they were all comparable from year to year. I was distraught over these battles and sought the Lord. I had never learned that familiar demonic spirits can attack and create the same negative things in your life over and over again.

I'm passionate about teaching others how to fight both mind-binding spirits and familiar spirits because I believe these are two seldom-discussed demonic entities. We must expose the enemy and how he works if we want to gain knowledge and freedom. If we don't know our opponent, we won't know how to combat him. As we expose him and his tactics, we move closer to freedom.

Familiar spirits send forth demonic assignments, known to us as warfare, emotional distress, and physical attacks. They create the same negative incidents in your life.

Are you ever frustrated because no matter how hard you work to deal with financial lack, it seems as if money issues continue to arise? You are reading this book on *Mind Battles*, but how many previous books have you previously read on the same subject? How many times have you taken two steps forward and one step backward in pursuit of your freedom? I want to encourage you that familiar spirits could be one of the two missing elements I will discuss in this book that could prevent your breakthrough. The other is mind-binding spirits, which I will discuss in chapter seven.

> **WHEN WE TAKE THE KNOWLEDGE WE GAIN AND PARTNER WITH THE HOLY SPIRIT, WE CAN RENEW OUR MINDS TO CANCEL AND DESTROY EVERY DEMONIC ATTACK.**

Victory comes through knowledge and prophetic insights. When we take the knowledge we gain and partner with the Holy Spirit, we will receive revelation, interpretation, impartation, and application. It will assist us to release our authority and renew our minds to cancel and destroy every demonic attack and hindrance sent our way. The gates of hell cannot prevail against us. (See Matthew 16:18.)

IN THE SPIRIT REALM

The demonic realm works to wreak havoc as it carries out its varied assignments like an army. Each demonic spirit has a specific function. Familiar spirits work together with monitoring spirits that observe and gather information.

Scripture tells us:

> *For our fight is not against flesh and blood, but against principalities, against powers, against the rulers of the darkness of this world, and against spiritual forces of evil in the heavenly places.* (Ephesians 6:12)

As I discuss in my book *Prophetic Spiritual Warfare*,[3] the demonic hierarchy is committed, organized, and disciplined.

---

3. Kathy DeGraw, *Prophetic Spiritual Warfare* (Lake Mary, FL: Charisma House, 2021).

Annihilating mind battles comes from knowing how the enemy wants to attack you in your mind through your emotions.

THE ENEMY USES WHAT YOU FEAR

As we look at the demonic realm and study its operation, it's important to note that not everything is a demon or a spiritual warfare attack. We live in an imperfect world. We can be out on the road and get a flat tire. We can run into a cashier who's not particularly nice. But how do we know when we're dealing with the demonic rather than something breaking because it's old and worn out or a person causing us grief because they're unhappy? We have to determine each situation, what emotions or feelings arise from within, and the root cause of the attack.

The enemy would cause fear to arise within me whenever my vehicle started to make weird noises. Monitoring spirits observe what makes you fear and will use that area of your life to attack you. Why do you think you can't get free from the thing you repeatedly struggle against? Because they are familiar with what makes you feel an unhealthy or unproductive emotion. Not only do they see how you respond, but they hear anything you say about the situation.

Proverbs 18:21 tells us, *"Death and life are in the power of the tongue."* As we speak out fear over objects and circumstances, the enemy will take note and produce curses in our life. The Bible tells us that our words have power. (See Psalm 19:14; Matthew 15:11; Ephesians 4:29, 5:4; 1 Peter 3:10.)

> AS WE SPEAK OUT FEAR OVER OBJECTS AND CIRCUMSTANCES, THE ENEMY WILL TAKE NOTE AND PRODUCE CURSES IN OUR LIFE.

I would talk to my husband about my vehicle and what I thought might be wrong. My fear came out in the natural as I talked about a certain noise or clicking, and the fear went forth in the spiritual, causing a natural event and mental torment. It created more warfare attacks against my vehicle and my mind; I was not being delivered of fear or worry in the process. Half the time, my vehicle actually had an issue, but the rest of the time, my imagination was activating because I was hypersensitive about anything regarding my vehicle.

The battle in this situation was twofold. First, I was experiencing spiritual warfare in my mind from the enemy, causing me to fear. Second, I was contributing to the problem by not casting my thoughts down. Instead, I allowed the fear to consume me. Rather than focusing on the positive—the vehicle was still running, and I didn't have an accident—I was consumed by the idea that there might be something wrong.

The enemy used this to his advantage to keep me in fear and full of worry. As I mentioned in a previous chapter, I was leaving for a ministry trip in Louisiana when the Lord told me my vehicle would break down three times before I returned. The first attack happened four hours outside of my hometown when my temperature gauge went into the red. Out in the middle of nowhere, there happened to be a repair shop with mechanics who were Pentecostal pastors. They blew air bubbles out of the line, and we got back on the road.

We didn't make it too far when the gauge ended up in the red again. We found another shop, and they couldn't find anything wrong. They consulted with a dealership, which suggested changing the thermostat. We changed it out due to the length of our trip, and then after ten days, four hours from home, the thermostat was in the red again. We stopped at a dealership, but the mechanic there didn't find anything wrong. He couldn't get it to overheat or go into the red again.

I was adamant that the gauge had repeatedly gone into the red. The mechanic ran every test he could think of and finally proved to me that the vehicle was not overheating. I looked at the mechanic and asked, "Do you believe in demons?"

Familiar spirits create repeated spiritual attacks along the same course of action. There was no other explanation for my vehicle to repeatedly overheat like that.

We must learn to identify familiar spirits and frequent disruptive incidents in order to know how to pray effectively to thwart the attacks and have peace during them. I know someone who puts a smiley face sticker over their check engine light so fear doesn't manifest when the light comes on. However, check engine lights can be warnings we need to heed. Ignorance is not bliss, whether it's a check engine light or spiritual warfare. We cannot prevent the war if we don't know it exists.

> IGNORANCE IS NOT BLISS, WHETHER IT'S A CHECK ENGINE LIGHT
> OR SPIRITUAL WARFARE. WE CANNOT PREVENT THE WAR
> IF WE DON'T KNOW IT EXISTS.

FINANCIAL ATTACKS

Just like Paul's thorn in the flesh that dealt him blow after blow (see 2 Corinthians 12:7–9), familiar spirits attack with what they have observed, where you fear, the special times in your life, and where you struggle to gain victory.

Familiar spirits can stop you from getting ahead financially no matter what you do. You pay your bills, give tithes and offerings, and spend your money wisely, but you're just getting by. Every time you take two steps forward, you take one step back. The battle can manifest in different ways, such as repeatedly getting laid off from work, paying off your bills only to have something break down so you have an unexpected expense, or having money coming in that never seems to be quite enough. The enemy is trying to discourage you through financial lack. When things like this happen repeatedly, a familiar spirit could be attacking to steal your peace, make you feel overwhelmed, and even get you frustrated with God.

HEALTH AILMENTS

Multiple medical conditions, chronic sickness, accidents, and injuries can all signify the work of a familiar spirit. There can be a spirit of sabotage against your prophetic destiny and a spirit of death assigned to your life. If you have dealt with physical infirmities multiple times, I encourage you to pay attention and see if a curse is at work in your life. Discern if a familiar spirit attacks you repeatedly or if you have hypochondriac tendencies, making you abnormally anxious about your health. Again, we cannot blame everything on a demon; there are times when we need to take responsibility for our feelings and overreactions. But we must look at the components of spiritual warfare.

Our son had to be resuscitated twice when he was born. I believe the enemy had an assignment on his life. Every year for twelve years, he had to go to the emergency room for a freak accident or something unusual. Then I discovered that there could be a curse at work in his life—a curse from familiar spirits that was activated at his birth. Once we prayed against the familiar spirits and accidents we saw manifesting in his life, the curse was broken. Our son has not been to the hospital since then, and he is now twenty-nine years old. He rarely visits the doctor either.

Familiar spirits make us anxious about our health. We begin to think we will never be well and never get healed. These demonic spirits attempt to continue the warfare, so we feel fatigued, victimized, and defeated. This is a plan of the enemy to steal, kill, and destroy your mind, leaving you fearful, depressed, and stressed.

RELATIONSHIPS

The enemy can use a person to bring warfare into your life. He employs people through the strongholds and demonic spirits with which they struggle. Rejected people often reject people. You can feel the tension of offensive, irritable people because they will often sow discord and disunity. Emotionally unhealthy people can harm your own emotions and contribute to your struggles.

Our emotions can and will be affected by those around us. Positive people who are filled with gratitude can benefit us and become a good influence in our spiritual walk and life.

You can evaluate your relationships by looking at your past or even the current influence of people in your life. As you think about people you know or have known, can you see any repeated broken relationships over the years that resulted in the same emotional ailment such as a feeling of rejection or a lack of control? Consider the character of these people. Did the relationship sever because they were repeatedly controlling you or rejecting you? If you can diagram multiple relationships that ended in the same sort of way, you could have a familiar spirit attacking to discourage you, waste your time, and steal your destiny.

> IF YOU CAN DIAGRAM MULTIPLE RELATIONSHIPS THAT
> ENDED IN THE SAME SORT OF WAY,
> YOU COULD HAVE A FAMILIAR SPIRIT ATTACKING YOU.

Ministry relationships are another area where we can frequently identify a demonic stronghold. Attacks can occur in churches where people suffer strife such as offense, pride, and rejection. If you analyze conversations and situations, you may discover commonalities in a particular person or ministry. Is one person hopping from church to church and causing problems, or are there challenges in the leadership that need to be addressed? People get focused on blaming a person when they should take a step back and discern the spiritual realm. What are the roots of the control or offense? Instead of judging and criticizing a person when there are repetitive challenges, we should seek the Holy Spirit for a deeper understanding of what is happening in the spiritual and natural. We need His wisdom to open our spiritual eyes, which reveal more than our physical eyes.

DISCOVERING THE CYCLES

People will manifest different emotional strongholds that can attack relationships. Identifying these strongholds will assist you so that you can prevent relational conflict.

REJECTED PEOPLE

People who struggle with rejection have often had multiple relationships over the years in which they have been rejected. Rejection will manifest as a familiar spirit until we learn that our acceptance is in the Lord. The Lord is our friend. He is everything we need. Even when unfortunate circumstances occur and we want to lean toward rejection, it is ultimately rooted in our lack of identity in Christ. We continually give familiar spirits the means to control us until we discover what the Word of God says about us. It becomes difficult to walk out of rejection otherwise because there's also a mind-binding spirit at work that makes us believe the lies in our mind.

CONTROLLING JEZEBEL SPIRITS

Spirits of control and familiar spirits will penetrate relationships and church settings. We once pastored a church that had split almost four times before we started there. A demonic spirit was causing disunity and destruction, but it was never identified since it was a legalistic church that didn't recognize spiritual warfare. People were actively participating with witchcraft spirits in the region. These spirits repeatedly tried to take over and control churches, schools, events, and activities there. Their goal was to put a stranglehold on the region so that no one thought about God's plans for their lives.

EMOTIONAL STRONGHOLDS

When identifying emotional strongholds, feelings such as fear can be the result of a learned behavior pattern. Our emotions are triggered for fear or there's a place in our soul where we feel traumatized. It can also be provoked by a generational curse or soul tie, which can materialize as an evil spirit or demonic strongman. Fear comes forth because of something that happened to us; it's a defensive measure to be alert so that it doesn't happen again.

Fear as a familiar spirit will observe what you fear, like it did for me with my vehicle. It knew my reaction and sent forth demonic assignments. Warfare attacks in my mind would continue to play out in false scenarios and vain imaginations because I feared and couldn't capture the thought. It kept me in an endless cycle of fear until I discovered its operations. Our imagination will work alongside fear, and it will become a challenge if we don't know the difference between spiritual attacks and our mind wandering.

The enemy will use the same demonic target in different ways. Although fear attacked in a season against my mind and my thinking about my vehicle, it would expand to other areas, such as fear of finances and sickness. If we can't reel in our thoughts, they will spiral out of control, and fear will begin to attack in several areas. Once we open a door to fear, we need to close that door as fast as we can, or it will open many other doors, and our fight will be bigger than when it started.

> IF WE CAN'T REEL IN OUR THOUGHTS, THEY WILL SPIRAL OUT OF CONTROL, AND FEAR WILL BEGIN TO ATTACK IN SEVERAL AREAS.

IDENTIFY ATTACKS

Familiar spirits will attack in the area with which they are familiar; it could be emotional, medical, relational, financial, or some other aspect of life. Diving deeper into these attacks, we can discover that they will attack each person differently based on different seasons, special events or happenings in our life.

I want to break this down because this will be key in finding out how they attack you so you can pray effectively to break the attacks. Familiar spirits usually operate on a timeline. If you mark up your calendar each year, you can pinpoint what month or months they attack, or whether attacks occur around a particular season, holiday, anniversary, or some other event.

My husband, for example, once had a double hernia that occurred instantly. Years later during that same month, he fell off a ladder at work and shattered his wrist. He said he felt as if something pushed him off. When he made that statement, it made me realize that this was no mere coincidence, but a demonic attack. Then he had a second hernia another year around the same time. After that, I started to pray one month before that timeframe to bind and restrict familiar spirits. It has been years since my husband's last attack.

Familiar spirits used to attack me around a particular holiday. I would notice dissensions in relationships a few days beforehand. They were beyond spats—they were full-blown relational sabotages that ended in emotional devastation. Since this was a special holiday for me, the enemy was attempting to sow seeds of dissent to cause me emotional turmoil rather than celebration. When I saw the commonalities in these instances, I prayed offensively to prevent future attacks.

Take a moment to discern negative things that happen to you repeatedly during a particular month, holiday, or season. Do you get attacked with mind ailments around your birthday, anniversary, or another meaningful time of year? Do your finances get attacked in a particular month, or do you have accidents or injuries in a certain season? Make a note of the month or months in which you have experienced trouble on the calendar on the next page.

	2013	2014	2015	2016	2017	2018	2019	2020	2021	2022
Jan.										
Feb.										
Mar.										
Apr.										
May										
June										
July										
Aug.										
Sept.										
Oct.										
Nov.										
Dec.										

Pay attention to areas where you can't seem to get a complete breakthrough. It could be that you are experiencing unseen warfare, invisible forces of evil spirits that cause attacks on your life. Be aware and alert. Allow me to lead and guide you through some activations and exercises to expose the enemy and root out familiar spirits.

Timelining is a prophetic exercise that will help you find the root cause, the place, and the reason familiar spirits began to attack. In the next chapter, we will discuss timelining to assist you in removing, repenting, and revoking demonic rights to these attacks.

PROPHETIC ACTIVATION

IDENTIFY THE BATTLE

Can you think of something repeatedly happening in your life, such as rejection, fear, financial lack, or health ailments? What strongholds in your mind have been difficult to break? Have you noticed the same cycles happening? What negative thoughts occupy your mind, or where do you feel held back?

FORGIVE AND REPENT

Are there places you didn't trust the Father with your finances or trust Jesus to be your Healer? Are there unhealthy emotions that you have felt or released to others from which you need to repent? Repent for any repeated words, feelings, or actions that you have released.

Say this prayer of forgiveness aloud:

Jesus, please forgive me for holding unforgiveness against any person. Holy Spirit, reveal to me open areas of my life where there's sin and I'm not releasing love as I should. Remove them from my life. I forgive myself and receive Your forgiveness for lack of trust with You to be my Healer and Provider. I choose this day to repent, turn around, and change my thought life. I thank You for freedom and receive my liberation!

TARGET THE BATTLE AND BREAK AGREEMENT

I break agreement and command every familiar spirit to leave my life, finances, health, family, job, and ministry in Jesus's name. I am redeemed and freed from repeated curses and familiar spirits. I claim that the same negative things will no longer continue to manifest. I call forth my blessings, health, and finances, and say all demonic attacks cease, in Jesus's name. I am blessed in my mind, and I have the Holy Spirit as my Helper.

RELEASE DELIVERANCE

Jesus was in the ministry of deliverance and cast out evil spirits. You are walking out your mind bondage. One of the keys to getting free and staying free is to cast out the correlating spirit that could be manifesting. Pray audibly and command the spirits of lying, depression, worry, stress, anxiety, fear, mind-binding, and torment to leave. Command it: "Spirit of _____, I cast you out, in Jesus's name."

WARFARE PRAYER DECLARATIONS

+ I command breakthrough is here and I am not going to go through the same negative events.

+ I revoke every targeted plan against my destiny and utterly destroy familiar attacks against me.

+ I renounce any sin and participation in the natural to activate familiar spirits in my life.

+ I refuse to allow negative thoughts to penetrate my mind and attack my thinking.

+ I command the same cycles of destruction in my life, health, and finances to cease in the name of Jesus.

REMOVE THE BATTLE

We can create our warfare when we don't press through to our breakthrough. We can put ourselves in a place of emotional defeat and feeling victimized. Releasing the battles in our minds comes from recognizing the struggle. There is no shame or condemnation if we bring part of the battle on ourselves. There is freedom in the truth. We can't get free if we don't recognize our role.

Spend some time thinking and taking any responsibility you need for the battle you face. Are you creating repeated happenings in your life?

PROPHETIC APPLICATION

1. Pray targeted prayers six weeks before familiar times of attacks against you or a loved one physically and emotionally.

2. Write a ten-sentence offensive declaration proclaiming those attacks to cease and bind and restrict future attacks.

FREEDOM THOUGHT

Guard your words. Not every spiritual warfare attack or emotional struggle is meant to be spoken out. Don't give the enemy leverage to intensify your battle.

4

BREAK AGREEMENT AND RECEIVE FREEDOM

I've done thousands of individual prayer sessions for inner healing and deliverance. I started with two four-hour sessions with people due to the severity of expelling demons. However, I knew very little back then. I read books, worked in the John G. Lake Healing Rooms in our area, and observed a ministry doing six deliverance sessions. After that, I went full force into casting out demons.

My first session was like boot camp because it was one of the worst cases imaginable. I believe the Lord may assign difficult tasks first to deliverance ministers so that everything else after that seems simple. After getting hands-on experience in deliverance ministry by trying it and practicing it, I opened my heart to move prophetically with the Spirit, and the Holy Spirit gave me the keys to accelerated deliverance.

When I first received my prophetic calling, I fought it. But as I repented, accepted the prophetic call on my life, and saw how it could accelerate a deliverance session from eight hours to one hour, I was sold. The Holy Spirit took me even further as He prophetically revealed to me how to timeline a person's past for obstacles and accelerate their freedom within five minutes. Nothing compares to seeing a person come in with bondage and watching their countenance change as they go out set free!

UNFORGIVENESS IS A STUMBLING BLOCK

The stumbling block of unforgiveness is one of the main reasons we stay stuck in mind battles. We can't wrap our mind around the idea of letting go of the past hurt and releasing the offender of the pain they caused us. As long as our will is gripping unforgiveness, our minds will stay locked up. We need to allow our emotions to release it.

Jesus said if you forgive others for their sins, *"your heavenly Father will also forgive you"* (Matthew 6:14), and if you have something against your brother, lay down your gift and go make amends. (See Matthew 5:23–24.)

> WHEN SOMEONE IS EXPERIENCING FEAR, ANGER, OFFENSE, OR REJECTION, IF THEY CAN'T RECEIVE FREEDOM IN THEIR MIND, THERE'S USUALLY A FORGIVENESS ISSUE IN THEIR HEART.

I discovered that whether someone is experiencing fear, anger, offense, or rejection, if they can't receive freedom in their mind, there's usually a forgiveness issue in their heart. They think it's just a head issue, but the problem started in their heart, and there the battle remained. The Bible says, *"For out of the abundance of the heart the mouth speaks"* (Matthew 12:34). There is a correlation between the mind and the heart. Our soul is comprised of our mind, our will, and our emotions. A heart problem will likely lead to a mind problem.

ROADBLOCKS TO FREEDOM

Whether they are emotional, spiritual, or natural (in the flesh), roadblocks hinder our breakthroughs. Rather than getting past the situation by emotionally releasing the unfairness, grudges, rejection, or anger, we hang on to the entitlement or debt we feel we are owed. We can't receive freedom because we are holding ourselves in bondage.

I know a woman who fell into years of mental health challenges stemming from how she was emotionally treated and abused in her family. The rejection and unfairness released anger in her life. After years of depression, rejection, and a food disorder, she had suicidal thoughts and planned her demise. This woman witnessed everyone else's bondage, the dismal way her mother was treated, and her family's expectations. How she perceived what had happened and the feelings she took upon herself led to years of dealing with torment, anxiety, and depression—years of bondage.

The entry point for her was not being loved unconditionally. Her siblings were not treated as poorly as she was. She did nothing wrong, but her family used her to take care of their selfish needs, health afflictions, and hurts.

This wonderful woman of God is a Spirit-filled, tongue-talking Christian who continually extended forgiveness to her family and would attempt to lay down anger. She knows the Word and what she needs to do. However, being a loving person, she doesn't want to leave her mom to care for herself, so she is in a constant state of emotional abuse from family members she lives with. She forgives, releases anger, and is fine for a while...until a major emotional violation from the family triggers another episode. She takes in guilt and condemnation in her mind because she knows she should be better than this, but with continued emotional abuse comes a continual spiritual battle.

Depression and rejection are emotional strongholds in her life that have to be continually broken. The entry point and root cause of these strongholds were the unfair treatment and rejection she has experienced.

She has to renew her thinking constantly with the Word of God, worship, and being in the Lord's presence.

She knew the entry point of the bondage, which I call the starting point of her timeline. Praise God she has received much freedom so far. In fact, she recalls one occasion when we were in the prayer room, and she felt a demonic spirit leave when I touched her head. "I felt something physically leave my mind, and it made my thinking so much better," she says.

She is no longer suicidal or depressed. The demonic spirit left. Now she has to continually release forgiveness and not take in the unhealthy emotions. She is on her way to freedom, but freedom is a journey—one that is well worth walking out.

> WHETHER YOU ARE SUFFERING FROM EMOTIONAL OR MENTAL ISSUES OR EVIL SPIRITS, YOU HAVE TO CONTINUALLY RENEW YOUR MIND AND CAPTURE THE HURTFUL THOUGHT TO ELIMINATE THE ROADBLOCK.

Whether you are suffering from emotional or mental issues or evil spirits, the process to find freedom is similar. You have to continually renew your mind and capture the hurtful thought to eliminate the roadblock.

EMOTIONAL HURT CREATES SOUL WOUNDS

Unforgiveness left in our hearts will create a stronghold in our minds. Left unchecked, unforgiveness can create unhealthy feelings and a right to entitlements we want in the natural for an emotional problem. When we have been hurt, betrayed, rejected, or offended, we seek an apology and vindication for something that happened in the natural to release us from how we feel emotionally. Unforgiveness in our hearts affects how we think and handle situations. In order to free our minds, we must free our hearts.

How we feel, think, and act are all consequences of what we have experienced. In the natural, our circumstances form us in a way that's similar to a generational curse. If our parents raised us in anger or fear, we can become angry and fearful. When a pattern is learned or taught, it becomes who we are. The good news is we don't have to stay that way. The Bible says:

> Do not be conformed to this world, but be transformed by the renewing of your mind, that you may prove what is the good and acceptable and perfect will of God.   (Romans 12:2)

We have a fight or flight response in stress or danger that we sometimes use in our everyday life. If we don't run away from a situation, we may forcefully resist it by trying to assume control. One of the ways we do this is by shutting down our emotions about past abuses and traumas and controlling our reactions so that no one ever hurts us again.

When we don't extend forgiveness to those who have hurt us, it builds a wall around our hearts. We say, "I will never allow them to do this to me again." We don't want to be rejected, hurt, or traumatized, so we decide, "I am in control. I will hang onto this incident by stuffing it down in my soul as a reminder, so I don't allow it to happen again."

You can also push down your emotions as a way to ignore what happened in your past, but it really does affect you in the present.

Stuffing down our emotions is unhealthy. As children, some of us heard, "Don't cry," "Don't wear your feelings on your sleeve," "It's no big deal, so just ignore it," and similar unhelpful phrases. These are unhealthy patterns our parents taught us to minimize or ignore difficult situations.

If you have been taught to stuff your feelings down and not talk about them, stop it. It is not healthy. If you are hanging on to a hurt as a self-protective coping ability, release it, and allow God to be your protector.

FREEDOM APPLICATION

Let's stop now and address the hurts of our past that we have ignored and stuffed down inside our souls.

+ Acknowledge what feelings, trauma, emotional abuse, or mental fatigue you have experienced.

+ Ask the Holy Spirit to convict you so that any dark soul wounds can be healed and brought to the light.

+ Pray and ask Him to assist you in receiving conviction and dealing with hurt.

+ Forgive the person who didn't validate your feelings or do anything to acknowledge them.

+ Forgive yourself for keeping quiet and believing the lie that your feelings didn't matter.

+ Permit yourself to speak. Declare audibly, "I have a voice and I will use it. What I feel and what I have to speak do matter. I am important to God and valuable to people."

Even though we need to permit ourselves to speak, we need to seek the Holy Spirit so we know what to share. Much of our mind bondage can be from keeping our feelings to ourselves, not speaking about an unfair situation, or dealing with the way our parents raised us.

> FIND A BALANCE BETWEEN SPEAKING OUT YOUR FEELINGS AND HOLDING YOUR TONGUE. PERMIT YOURSELF TO SPEAK AS THE SPIRIT LEADS.

Find a balance between speaking out your feelings and holding your tongue. Permit yourself to speak as the Spirit leads. Address an issue by first going to the Holy Spirit and seeking Him for wisdom.

When we go to a person to help us solve our problems, their answers can become part of our mind battle. People can say fleshly things that can make us irritated and take in more offense. Be slow to speak and quick to listen.

TIMELINING HURT OF THE PAST

Our daughter had a rebellious attitude. She didn't get into trouble by participating in unclean activities or recreational substances, but she was defiant. When she went off to college, the Lord spoke to me three times on the drive there. He said, "This is My will for her life." That made it easier to let her go.

At a secular university, she began to transform and pursue Jesus and her liberation. She would come home, talk things out, and work on healing relationships.

Years of rejection and rebellion all emanated from a time we were pastoring. Our church split and rejected us. Our children lost all of their friends, not merely through people leaving but also through an intense battle of words and situations aimed directly at them. Within a year, her closest friend rejected her too. This made our daughter put up self-protective walls and not want to pursue God for years.

We went back through the years and timelined negative events, broken friendships, and when her relationships began to be affected. The entry point was being rejected at church. The root cause was she was hurt. The legal right was that she didn't want to let go of rebellion and release forgiveness. She was hurt, resented having to move, disliked being a pastor's kid, and wasn't ready to move forward. She had to live with a stronghold in her mind until the Holy Spirit led her away from home to a university, where she had to live in a college dorm, with a new church and a praying mama back home. You bet I attacked those spirits of rejection and rebellion in the spiritual realm. Four times I went into her bedroom and declared and took authority over evil spirits. My husband blew the shofar and twice declared with me. And then she began to change.

When she came home for the summer, she would work on one of the family relationships she had strained. She would pray and seek the Lord for deliverance; in the midst of this, her prophetic gift was activated. She went from being rebellious to going on mission trips, assisting in baptisms, doing street evangelism, living in a Christian women's house at college, and leading small groups. She's now married to a Christian, in a small group, and playing keyboard on her worship team. God transformed her through the renewing of her mind! She had to digest and work through the battle in her mind before she could walk out in freedom.

TIMELINING FOR SELF-DELIVERANCE

Timelining is prophetically allowing the Holy Spirit to reveal the past through supernatural revelation, using natural and spiritual abilities to partner with Him to break strongholds and release freedom. As you engage with the Spirit, you rely on His wisdom, counsel, and understanding to move you through the revelatory process quickly.

There are many functions in which we can depend on the Holy Spirit to increase our discernment. Operating with the seven spirits of the Lord upon me (see Isaiah 11:2) took me from eight-hour deliverance sessions to one hour. When discerning a specific issue in someone's life with the Holy Spirit's counsel, I can pinpoint a direct cause and entry point within five minutes. It is an acceleration in the person's deliverance as the Holy Spirit will reveal the hurt inside them and the blockage they have set up in their mind that prevents freedom. When I embraced the prophetic, the Holy Spirit would show me a vision or tell me what happened to someone so that I could see the wounds of their heart.

TIMELINING EXAMPLE

Here is an example of timelining to assist you with this practice, which leads to discovering the root cause.

A familiar spirit of rejection has been following a woman throughout her life. She is now forty-five and suffering from an emotional ailment, unable to receive freedom. We want to see if we can identify the root cause of this rejection, and what is giving it its legal right. This woman is also experiencing control and rejection from a present friendship.

Here are questions I would ask to move backward and quickly find the entry point prophetically.

1. How long have you been in this relationship and experiencing rejection? Eight years

2. Before this, have you ever felt rejected? Yes

3. When? At age thirty

4. Who rejected you? My sister

5. Did you forgive her? Yes

6. Did you feel rejected before your sister? Yes

7. Did you suffer rejection in your teen years? Yes

8. Did you forgive your friend who rejected you in your teen years? No

Here we can see that there is an open door to rejection and unforgiveness that has followed her as a familiar spirit. It is still manifesting years later. This is one of the main reasons people struggle. Rejection is a common mind battle. Unless the ministry of forgiveness is released, the mind torment will continue.

In my book *Unshackled*, I lead people through forgiveness and inner healing. In timelining to find the entry point, we have to equally root out unforgiveness and heal the emotional soul wounds such as offense, anger, control, and rejection.

FREEDOM APPLICATION

Let's try to identify an issue in your life where you haven't been able to receive a breakthrough.

+ What is one area in which you haven't been able to receive a breakthrough, such as an emotional ailment or physical infirmity?

+ Is there something you have prayed to be removed from your life that you still struggle with?

+ What are the three biggest things holding you back from the fullness of God?

+ What negatively consumes your mind?

Now looking at the timeline below, mark when the issue started. Using the format I have suggested, keep going back until you find your entry point on the timeline. Write it down so you know what you are dealing with and when.

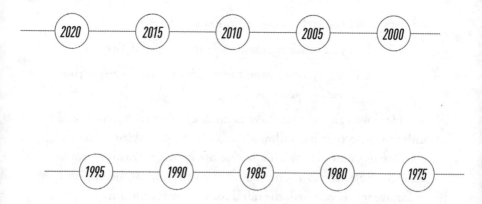

FIND YOUR ENTRY POINT

What is holding you back from the fullness of God? Why haven't you been able to receive freedom? Ask yourself what happened six to eighteen months before that incident. Was there hurt or trauma? Have you healed from that?

Now let's go deeper, looking back five or ten years to see if there's anything that resembles the issue you just discerned. Ask yourself, "How do I feel about that situation? Have I forgiven? Am I fine with it?" Keep going backward in five- or ten-year increments until you can't find anything else.

When partnering with the Holy Spirit, this should only take about five minutes to find the root cause and legal right to the familiar spirit. Quickly go back, identify the source, make sure you've dealt with it, and then move forward.

BREAKING AGREEMENT WITH STRONGHOLDS

Struggling with an issue for over five, fifteen, or forty years creates a stronghold, a place we are bound in our minds and a negative area on which we focus. Over time, our brains can change and be transformed either positively or negatively. Even if we've been depressed for years, felt stress plague our minds, or responded adversely to fear, we don't have to stay that way.

These strongholds and behavior patterns truly become us if we let them. Stress, anxiety, depression, and worry attack us. We agree with these negative emotions, not willingly, but by acting and reacting to the attacks and taking in the feelings. Our brain becomes trained to respond in certain ways as it copes with adversity.

> OUR BRAIN BECOMES TRAINED TO RESPOND IN CERTAIN WAYS
> AS IT COPES WITH ADVERSITY. WE CAN CHANGE OUR BRAIN INSTEAD
> OF LETTING OUR CIRCUMSTANCES CHANGE IT.

Our mind is a powerful tool. God created our brain to be neuroplastic and malleable, so that it can adapt and change. He gave us the ability to easily influence, train, and control our thoughts. Even if we've been fearful for a long time, we can change our brain to revert to thoughts of peace instead of letting our circumstances dictate what goes on in our heads.

However, many people are stuck in bondage because they don't believe change is possible. They become what has attacked them and fall into victimhood or defeatist mentalities. They may also be afraid that they won't be themselves without their emotional ailments or circular thoughts—what I call *the junk in their trunk*.

It is difficult to pull your mind back into a positive direction when you have been bound for so long. I find it extremely comforting to know that your brain can change. It truly is good news!

You can be released from shame, guilt, and condemnation. Romans is a good place to begin to renew your mind.

Romans 8:1 says, "*There is therefore now no condemnation for those who are in Christ Jesus, who walk not according to the flesh, but according to the Spirit.*" Pull on your spirit man when your mind seems to be going in an unproductive direction. Focus on the Holy Spirit within you and say, "Holy Spirit, I can't do this in my strength. Will You help me refocus my mind?" Romans 12:2 says, "*Do not be conformed to this world, but be transformed by the renewing of your mind.*" You are not fear. You are not rejection. You are not condemnation. You are not depression. It is not the way God wired you and created you to be.

Natural circumstances brought forth unhealthy emotions and torment, but it is not who you are. You may have changed your thinking because of things that happened to you, but you didn't purposefully do it. Your brain was rewired because you took things in and processed them in an unhealthy way. You did not make yourself depressed. Your brain changed because of your circumstances. But the Bible is the good news, and the good news is that we are new in Christ!

> *Therefore, if any man is in Christ, he is a new creature. Old things have passed away. Look, all things have become new.*
> (2 Corinthians 5:17)

In Christ, we have a new mind and a fresh beginning, but the turnaround begins with you. It starts with you renewing and reprogramming your brain. It starts with you making a daily choice to think positive thoughts. It begins with you *"casting down imaginations and...bringing every thought into captivity"* (2 Corinthians 10:5) and replacing it with a truth found in God's Word.

We have a responsibility to capture our thoughts. Stinking thinking will get us nowhere. We have something to do about our situation. We may have fallen victim to our circumstances, but we are wired to change, not stay that way. Negative occurrences may have changed our brain, but Father God wired us to be positive. Our brain is malleable and pliable. This is good news because now we can change it to how Father God intended us to be!

PROPHETIC ACTIVATION

IDENTIFY THE BATTLE

Can you see a difference between how your mind used to think and how it thinks currently? What changed and could be the root of it? Have you been so intense in your schedule that your mind is constantly running rampant? How can you adjust your schedule and control your thoughts to achieve balance?

FORGIVE AND REPENT

As you timeline the current issue for which you seek emotional healing, is there someone you need to forgive? Is there a name that comes back to your soul occasionally? When you hear a name that's similar to the name of the person who hurt you, does it bring back repressed feelings? Is this a word of knowledge the Holy Spirit is giving you that there are still soul wounds with that person?

Pray audibly this prayer of forgiveness:

Holy Spirit, I give You permission to convict me and bring anyone and everyone I need to forgive into God's light. I repent of unforgiveness in my heart. I rebuke the need for retribution or retaliation. I know You are the judge and vindicator. I release forgiveness to those who have hurt me and I forgive myself for any shame, condemnation, or regret I am holding on to, in Jesus's name. Amen.

TARGET THE BATTLE AND BREAK AGREEMENT

I proclaim and declare, I break agreement with every hindering spirit and wrong thought. I come out of agreement with a victim mentality and lack of ambition to pursue God's presence and my deliverance. I break agreement and sever ungodly soul ties with unhealthy relationships. I command my emotions to align with the Word of God and declare that by Christ's stripes, I am healed, in Jesus's name. Amen!

RELEASE DELIVERANCE

Jesus was in the ministry of deliverance and cast out evil spirits. You are walking out your mind bondage now. One of the keys to getting free and staying free is to cast out the correlating spirit that could be manifesting. Pray audibly and command any of the following spirits to leave: lying, depression, worry, stress, anxiety, fear, mind-binding, torment, unforgiveness, and offense. Declare, "Spirit of _____, I cast you out, in Jesus's name."

WARFARE PRAYER DECLARATIONS

+ I obstruct every plan of the enemy to sabotage my relationships and cause me repeated offense and rejection.

+ I paralyze the powers of darkness coming against my mind, and I declare I think good thoughts!

+ I extinguish every flaming dart of the enemy and burn up the blueprints of hell against my mind.

+ I desecrate and damage every demonic assignment causing my mind confusion.

+ I take authority over every wrong thought. I cast out everything that does not align with God's Word.

REMOVE THE BATTLE

What type of ownership have you taken in your mind that you need to rebuke, dismiss, and cast out? Have you accepted the attitude of a victim or someone who's been defeated? Have you labeled yourself as depressed, mentally ill, or demonically oppressed? You possess what you confess. Renewing your mind requires a positive confession from your mouth. Where can you change your words and how you think of yourself to align with the new sound mind God is giving you?

PROPHETIC APPLICATION

1. Timeline one of your emotional ailments or physical infirmities to see if you can discover your entry point, root cause, and legal right.

2. Practice your discernment and allow the Holy Spirit to move through you. Do the timeline exercise with a friend or family member to assist them to freedom. Purchase a copy of this book for them.

FREEDOM THOUGHT

You have to look back to move forward. Don't get stuck in the trauma. Simply identify the root cause so you can move up and forward to conquer the issue.

5

STOP FEAR

A generational curse kept me bound in fear for forty years. To me, fear was a normal reaction to everyday life. After being taught to fear and think the worst, I didn't realize I could be free from that negativity. I knew nothing about deliverance. Many demons of fear manifested in my life, such as fear of financial and health issues, darkness, driving over a bridge with water underneath, heights, and storms. Fear was an emotional stronghold; in some cases, it was also a demonic strongman.

The torment would be so consuming that I sometimes could not pull my mind back toward good and God for up to thirty-six hours. I didn't live with fear every minute as some people do, feeling as if they are constantly on edge, but when fear attacked, it would grip me, and I could feel it manifest physically. I liken it to being emotionally paralyzed. I could feel fear rise from within, and I knew I had to evict it once and for all.

When I was prostrate on the floor for two years as I sought the Lord, He began to teach and instruct me. In the process, I learned that I was bound to emotional fear, and I didn't need to live like that. The torment I was suffering was not God's intention for me.

My husband couldn't understand how fear could paralyze me and affect my mind so much. He had no comprehension of fear, worry, and torment like I experienced. There were several times when I had to push through and pray like never before. If only I had had the tenacity to pray like I do now and kick fear out of my mind! Sadly, I often let fear get the best of me instead. Yet it is in those moments of fear that what we do matters most.

ACTION NOT A REACTION

As fear and torment manifested, it would shut me down. In *Divergent*,[4] one of my favorite movies, one of the main characters tells another, "Fear doesn't shut you down. It wakes you up." I don't want fear to shut me down. I want it to crank me up and wake me up to put the devil under my feet. I want to be unmovable, unshakable, and fearless. Fear can and does shut us down, just as anxiety, depression, and worry do, but we have nothing to fear. God's Word tells us:

> *Don't be afraid, for I am with you; don't be distressed, for I am your God. I give you strength, I give you help, I support you with my victorious right hand.* (Isaiah 41:10 CJB)

Fear contributes to worry, stress, and anxiety. As we look at the root of fear, we see it is intertwined with many emotional ailments.

How it affects and attacks you is specific to you. When you think about fear, what does it do to you internally? How does it aggravate you and make you feel? What causes torment?

> FEAR CAN TORMENT US WITH THOUGHTS THAT SOMETHING BAD FROM OUR PAST WILL OCCUR AGAIN. THEN A FAMILIAR SPIRIT AND A MIND-BINDING SPIRIT KEEP THE FEAR IN OPERATION.

Fear can torment us with thoughts that something bad from our past will occur again. This fear brings forth a familiar spirit and a mind-binding spirit, keeping it in operation. Our minds can

---

4. *Divergent*, directed by Neil Burger (2014; Lionsgate).

begin to have vain imaginations and ruminate, creating a cycle of fear.

I was bound by such a fear of accidents that even when I wasn't in the car, I was still imagining car accidents. My mind became trapped in that fear. It didn't matter if it was a demonic spirit or my thoughts, it was still fear.

You have to identify how your mind battle plays out and manifests when it is a spirit versus your flesh, how to tell the difference, and how to conquer the different manifestations, feelings, and emotions.

SIMPLIFY THE BATTLE

Our mind is a battlefield—creative, intelligent, and full of thoughts and feelings. One of the ways we can take victory over mind battles is by simplifying the struggle.

I'm going to use an example that you may relate to so that you can get freedom. I used to take prescription medication for high blood pressure. When I had to see the doctor for my yearly checkup, I was all fearful about my blood pressure. Fear raised my levels, and I would have to wait five or ten minutes until I calmed down to have it taken again. I was allowing fear to arise. It wasn't a demon of fear. It was fear, anxiety, and worry I allowed to occur within me.

It was not only a physical generational curse, but also an emotional generational curse. I was told things like, "Don't eat too much salt; it'll give you high blood pressure," or "When you have high blood pressure, you can have a heart attack." I often had to talk myself out of fear. It was a tool I gave myself to help minimize unhealthy emotions.

In the case of having my blood pressure taken, I would say to myself, "You are getting all worked up over a piece of material going around your arm." I didn't allow myself to think further than that. I didn't think about the blood pressure cuff producing a reading. I would just think about it as a piece of material, which helped me to conquer the fear. I would also listen to music in my earbuds to keep me in a place of peace.

Over the years, I got off all high blood pressure medicine, and I'm no longer afraid to have my readings taken. I had to simplify the mind battle in order to conquer it. I rebuked word curses from the doctors that I would live with high blood pressure and need multiple medications. I broke generational curses that health problems would plague me.

FREEDOM APPLICATION

What battle do you face and fear? Where and how can you minimize the fear?

_____

_____

_____

_____

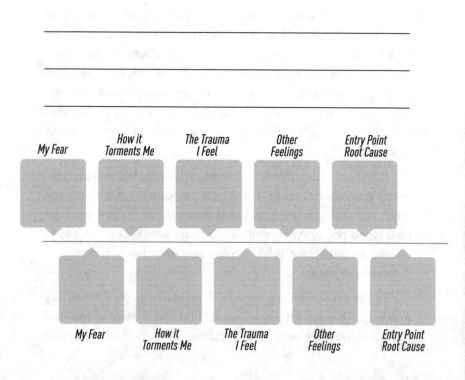

Let's chart out your fear. On the previous page, jot down what makes you fear, the trauma you experience, and how it torments you. Keep going until you can't find any other root cause or emotional effect. See if you can discover the ultimate reason why you fear so you can remove it. Can you simply your battle as I did with my fear regarding my blood pressure?

THE AUTHOR OF CONFUSION

The devil is the author of confusion. Confusion, fear, and torment exist together, along with familiar spirits and mind-binding spirits. If the enemy can confuse you, he can emotionally torment and paralyze you.

> THE DEVIL IS THE AUTHOR OF CONFUSION. IF HE CAN CONFUSE YOU, HE CAN EMOTIONALLY TORMENT AND PARALYZE YOU.

When you're persecuted in a mind battle, you become trapped in an endless cycle in which you cannot hear the Lord. As fear attempts to invade your life, your thought process is hindered; everything that appears to be normal has just been disrupted in the spiritual realm.

Even when you are accustomed to hearing from the Lord, the fear will confound your discernment. Suddenly, the simplicity with which you normally hear God becomes chaos. Fear doesn't want you operating in faith. If it can attack you with confusion, it can make you doubt whether you are clearly hearing from the Lord. Where confusion exists, the enemy is attempting to penetrate. In order to discern whether there's a spirit of fear at work or if the fear is simply a normal human response to a terrible situation, you need to evaluate the level of confusion and the means by which the fear attacks.

Confusion is never of the Lord. In the times when this kind of fear and torment are oppressing you, take a step back, breathe, redirect your thoughts, step aside, and do something else for a moment to refocus. Distract yourself in another direction by doing something you enjoy that's beneficial, like listening to soothing music, going for a walk, or reading a good book. Spend time in the presence of the Lord. When you are in fear, removing yourself from the situation can help you regain your composure and press through to your breakthrough.

CONDITIONED TO FEAR

Fear exists to keep us safe. Our central nervous system conditions us to fear—a survival instinct designed to protect us from danger and impending harm. When we fear, adrenaline is released, which causes our heart to race and pump more blood to our muscles. Fear can fill us with the energy to exhibit supernatural strength in emergency situations. It can also release serotonin, which helps our brains work more efficiently.

God created fear to protect us, give us energy, and help us react and act. It is a gift from God that's designed to be advantageous to us in a crisis. However, the enemy has disrupted our fear with a mind battle and turned it into a disadvantage.

We have to embrace fear. For years, I've been telling people, "Don't resist the process and what you experience. Leaning into the obstacle as it occurs will enable you to conquer it easier."

I'm not saying embrace your struggle to the extent that you're exclaiming, "Oh, goodie, this is happening to me!" However, instead of resisting what you are feeling and experiencing, stay there with it. For example, if the Lord is dealing with you on the issue of rejection, instead of fighting the deliverance because you know it will be hard and hurtful, embrace it. Accept that you need to work through rejection even if it is difficult.

God has wired us to fear as a defense mechanism. It pumps adrenaline and gives us brain power to think and strength in our bodies, all of which is designed to keep us from harm. We need to take all that fear produces in the negative, group those things together, and use them to our advantage. All of those adverse fearful feelings can give us the adrenaline and strength to pull out of the mind battle. Instead of caving in to the negative emotions of fear and allowing them to bind us, we need to use the force with which God naturally designed us to rise and pray, declare and decree, hammer out fear, and put the devil under our feet. We need to release that adrenaline to pray and declare, "Fear doesn't shut me down; it cranks me up and calls me to action." Let's put the devil under our feet and not allow him to take something God intended for good and turn it into something bad.

> GOD HAS WIRED US TO FEAR AS A DEFENSE MECHANISM.
> THE ADRENALINE INDUCED BY FEAR GIVES US BRAIN POWER TO THINK
> AND STRENGTH IN OUR BODIES.

We are three-part beings—soul, spirit, and physical body. God has created each part of us to engage in the battle. When we engage our three-part being, we can pull ourselves out of the fight. Since God has made our natural body to produce strength and make our brain work more effectively in times of fear, we can use this to our advantage.

Some people may become stuck in a mind battle because they don't know how to free themselves. When the attacks come, we need to draw on what God has naturally given us to move forward out of the attack. We need to take the natural energy He has given us and use that as a means to get up and pray. We need to take advantage of our brain working more effectively during those fearful times to discern our situation and pull ourselves forward when we don't feel as if we can. Instead of allowing the torment to paralyze us emotionally, we must take what is naturally happening and put it to good use.

Therefore, as the adrenaline is pumping and the serotonin is releasing, use that opportunity to put your emotions into alignment with what is happening physically so you can pray, pull yourself out of depression, and smash fear. As you use your body to engage in the warfare, your emotions will change and come into alignment. Then spiritually, you will be able to stand, fight, and win the battle!

RESIST FEAR CONDITIONING

Fear conditioning is a negative response that causes us to learn to fear certain situations. If we are raised to fear specific things, we could be dealing with a generational curse. Natural occurrences, people, conversations, media, and medical doctors can all fear condition us. We get conditioned to fear by what people say, how they act, or how their words or actions affect us. This fear conditioning must be rooted out of us so that we don't pass it onto others.

The Lord showed me a vision of people running chaotically in the streets. I saw buildings coming down and destruction everywhere. People in the streets were frantic and in need of medical assistance. The Lord told me that something was going to happen and that I needed to root out fear so I could be in faith.

We want to be witnesses on the earth, but how can we do that if we are in fear? How can we be contagious Christians if we are living in fear? We can't. In times of destruction, we can't assist others if we haven't helped ourselves. Before every airplane takes off, the flight attendants tell us that in an emergency, we must put our own oxygen masks on first before assisting others. In a similar fashion, we need to evict our own fear so that we can help others in crisis.

The Lord revealed to me there is a principality of fear in operation over the earth. It manifests as fear of sickness, fear of finances, fear of end times, and fear of lack. The Lord showed me that the principality of fear gains strength when we don't root the individual fear out of ourselves. We need to evict fear from our lives so that we aren't releasing it and exuding it onto other people. When we all hold onto individual fear, it fuels the principality of fear over the earth. Fear is contagious.

> A PRINCIPALITY OF FEAR IN OPERATION OVER THE EARTH MANIFESTS AS FEAR OF SICKNESS, FEAR OF FINANCES, FEAR OF END TIMES, AND FEAR OF LACK.

What are you doing to contain your fear?

Fear conditioning comes through conversations at church, messages preached on the pulpit, news spread by the media, financial market fluctuations, plague predictions, and natural happenings. These fear contributors ultimately release control in and over our lives. As we are impacted by another person's fear, events, and news, it becomes a form of fear conditioning over us. Fear of what we hear restricts our movements, and people in authority release fear that ultimately controls our minds. (See chapter eight for more on how fear traps us in control.)

If we want to be set free from fear, we need to see all aspects of it. We need to guard what we put in our soul and spirit. If people around us are instilling fear, it is our choice to remove ourselves from those interactions to protect ourselves. When we are struggling to receive freedom from mind battles, we don't need other people contributing to them.

If listening to the news causes you to fear, then spend time listening to God instead. If you have people in your life who make you feel weighed down after conversing with them, you may need to take a break from them while you get your mind under control. Don't allow fear to control your life. Grab hold of it before it takes hold of you!

As I was trying to gain freedom in my own mind, I had to choose what conversations I would allow into my soul. Sometimes I would be listening to someone on the phone and hear something that triggered fear in me. I learned to pull the phone away from my ear for a few moments. Then I would check back on the conversation to see if they had moved on. I had to guard what came into my soul. Otherwise, the fear that came in would control my mind and cause my thoughts or actions to go in a negative direction.

PROPHETIC ACTIVATION

IDENTIFY THE BATTLE

Everyone has a battle that they face. Yours is specific to you. Although others may experience something similar, it's not the same as your battle. Carefully identify your battle as it correlates to fear. What is the trauma or torment that is driving fear in your life?

FORGIVE AND REPENT

The fear you experience could be a result of another person's fear, trauma, a world event, or a situation that happened in your life due to something someone did or said to you. Think about your fear for a moment. Figure out what it stems from and then release forgiveness to another.

Pray audibly this prayer of forgiveness:

Heavenly Father, I choose today to forgive anyone who has contributed to the fear I experience. I release them to You, Jesus, and I forgive them in my heart and mind. I repent of fear that I have taken in and I destroy its hold on me, in Jesus's name.

TARGET THE BATTLE AND BREAK AGREEMENT

Speak out and decree:

I speak and establish that I break agreement with fear and proclaim that I will control my thoughts. When people talk negatively and in fear, I will counteract by speaking positively and declaring faith. I command that I have not been given a spirit of fear but love, power, and a sound, self-disciplined, and self-controlled mind. By the blood of Jesus, I break agreement with every mind battle and destroy the enemy's power in my life causing fear.

RELEASE DELIVERANCE

Jesus was in the ministry of deliverance and cast out evil spirits. You are walking out your mind bondage. One of the keys to getting free and staying free is to cast out the correlating spirit that could be manifesting, such as a spirit of lying, depression, worry, stress, anxiety, fear, mind-binding, or torment. Pray audibly and command the spirit to leave: "Spirit of _____, I cast you out, in Jesus's name."

WARFARE PRAYER DECLARATIONS

+ I destroy every mind-binding spirit of fear and torment that has been sent on assignment to me.

+ I rebuke and utterly cut off every fearful spirit from my childhood and my past in Jesus's name.

+ I repent and release every fearful thought plaguing my mind and permeating my heart.

+ I refuse to allow fear to control me. I will no longer succumb to fear. Get out of me in Jesus's name.

+ I abort every plan of the enemy to steal, kill, and destroy my thoughts and take something God meant for good and torment me with it. I will not live in fear, but faith!

REMOVE THE BATTLE

Establish a battle plan of how to capture and remove your fearful thoughts. One of the ways to remove the battle is to fill yourself up with Scripture so that you have powerful proclamations to speak out to counterattack everything from the enemy. You have the power to remove the battle when you rely on the Holy Spirit. Ask Him for your specific battle plan.

PROPHETIC APPLICATION

1. Choose your words wisely. What words can you remove from your vocabulary to minimize fear?

2. After Job lost everything, he said, *"The thing which I greatly feared has happened to me, and that which I dreaded has come to me"* (Job 3:25). Where do you need to renew your mind, so your fearful thoughts don't become a reality?

FREEDOM THOUGHT

You were wired for fear. Use it to your advantage instead of allowing the enemy to use it to your disadvantage.

6

CAPTURE EVERY THOUGHT

No one ever taught me how to capture every thought and make my thoughts obedient to Christ as Scripture tells us in 2 Corinthians 10:5. I didn't have anyone to mentor me on this, and the church I attended didn't teach it. So fear would torment me. Vain imaginations manifested and false scenarios would play out in my mind. No matter how many books I read, I couldn't find one that truly helped with mind battles, particularly when it came to capturing fearful thoughts that galloped through my brain. Instead of dismissing the thought, I would entertain it. It would plague my mind while I was on my way to speak at conferences, when I was alone at home, and even when I was supposed to be relaxing on vacation. I didn't have the tools to capture my thoughts, so I stayed in bondage.

Whether you struggle with fear, anxiety, rejection, anger, offense, or any other emotional stronghold, you can capture every thought. The information in this book can be used for every stronghold, including addiction, temptation, sin, and runaway emotions. They have one commonality: they are all a battle that plays a tug-of-war in your mind. But *you* can win the war!

DISMANTLE UNPRODUCTIVE AND UNFRUITFUL THOUGHTS

In the natural and in the spiritual realm, our minds can be lured into thinking in a particular direction. Our minds go to wandering thoughts 47 percent of the time[5] and can become stuck in rumination—a repetitive, negative thought process that loops continuously without end or completion.[6] Often distressing and difficult to stop, the pattern usually involves repeating a negative thought.

> OUR MINDS CAN BECOME STUCK IN RUMINATION—
> A REPETITIVE, NEGATIVE THOUGHT PROCESS THAT LOOPS
> CONTINUOUSLY WITHOUT END OR COMPLETION.

Our minds are also lured into repetitive negative thinking by mind-binding spirits. These evil spirits are both blinding and binding. They seduce us into focusing in a direction contrary to God's Word.

It can feel like an invisible force is locking your mind down so that the only thing you can think about is the pornography you are trying to avoid, the fear and torment you are trying to evict, the depression oppressing you to the point where you cannot function, and any number of issues that come from mind-binding spirits. These tormenting spirits will pull you into thinking about the very thing from which you are trying to obtain freedom. They are strongmen in the kingdom of darkness, the driving force behind every addiction, rejection, passivity, and mind bondage. If they are not exposed, you stay in bondage. The main keys to receiving deliverance from mind-binding spirits is to know they exist, take authority over them and cast them out, capture every thought, and renew your mind by reading the Word of God.

---

5. Alison Escalante, "New Science: Why Our Brains Spend 50% Of The Time Mind-Wandering," *Forbes*, January 28, 2021, www.forbes.com/sites/alisonescalante/2021/01/28/new-science-why-our-brains-spend-50-of-the-time-mind-wandering.
6. See Dina Scolan's article on rumination from the OCD & Anxiety Center, theocdandanxietycenter.com/rumination.

We need both emotional restoration and spiritual deliverance because mind and spiritual strongholds operate together. The struggle is partially due to lack of discipline to take control over our minds and not allow vain imaginations. Our minds are meant to be creative, but when they are not disciplined, we allow our thoughts to scatter and wander in different directions. The battlefield of the mind is intense, so we need to be intentional and focused in our thinking.

When we scroll through social media news feeds and online news, it becomes obvious that a lack of discipline is currently ruling our lives. We aren't obtaining concrete information, and yet we keep scrolling, training our brain to stay busy, making it harder to pull our thoughts in a positive direction. We have developed a pattern of scrolling through the Internet, allowing our minds to go here and there. It's unproductive and unfruitful, a waste of time that steals your destiny.

Trust me, I know about wandering thoughts! Just today, I was in prayer when my mind went off someplace else. I thought to myself, *Where is this coming from?* I had to consciously capture those thoughts and refocus my mind to return to concentrated prayer and spending time with my Lord. Even as I'm writing this book, I will research something and find my mind drawn to something else so that I have to reel it back in. I don't think any of us can prevent our minds from going off on tangents 100 percent of the time, but part of exposing the battle is revealing the truth of its operations, taking action to combat it, and redirecting ourselves.

Having a mind that isn't always focused in the direction it should be is a challenge in itself. Now, throw in a strong, mind-binding demonic spirit that's vying for your attention, pulling you into destructive thoughts, negativity, fear, and depression.

It is difficult enough to capture our thoughts by practicing to control them, but when an evil spirit is beguiling our thoughts into a direction contrary to our immediate purposes and pursuits, it can become a struggle to emerge victorious. The good news is that we now have exposed two types of enemies: evil spirits and our lack of self-control to discipline our thoughts.

What's the common denominator? It's us! Ouch! Yes, that's right. We have the power within us to both take authority over and cast out a demon and capture our thoughts. It takes work and effort, but we can do it!

SCRIPTURE GIVES US THE KEYS

There are two Scriptures that have been pertinent in my life for capturing and casting down every thought and renewing my mind to release mind bondage. Here's one of them:

> *For the weapons of our warfare are not carnal, but mighty through God to the pulling down of strongholds, casting down imaginations and every high thing that exalts itself against the knowledge of God, bringing every thought into captivity to the obedience of Christ.* (2 Corinthians 10:4–5)

The weapons we use are supernatural, not of human origin. We take the first action in the natural to acknowledge the thought, and then we cast it down. When we struggle in this area, we need to cry out to the Holy Spirit and ask Him for help. Seek conviction for when you need to cast down the thought.

> WE MUST PULL DOWN "EVERY HIGH THING THAT EXALTS ITSELF AGAINST THE KNOWLEDGE OF GOD."

We are to cast down imaginations—our mind and flesh—by taking action in the natural against what is happening. We must pull down *"every high thing that exalts itself against the knowledge of God."* We know this refers to demonic attacks; Satan thought so highly of himself that he fell from heaven. Any evil spirit that is penetrating your mind needs to be cast down and out.

Regarding the Scripture from 2 Corinthians, Finis Jennings Dake wrote, "Lascivious, vain and evil thoughts of all kinds are brought down and made obedient to His laws." I like the correlation between vain thoughts that are human and fleshy, and evil thoughts, which are spiritually demonic. It helps us to understand how we can be attacked on both fronts. Bringing down evil thoughts is contingent on us taking authority, which is dominion. According to *Strong's Concordance*, the Hebrew word for "dominion," *rāḏâ* (H7287), means to tread down, subjugate, have dominion, prevail against, reign, and rule.

> *God blessed them and said to them, "Be fruitful and multiply, and replenish the earth and subdue it. Rule over the fish of the sea and over the birds of the air and over every living thing that moves on the earth."*   (Genesis 1:28)

In Hebrew, the word translated here as "subdue" is *kāḇaš* (*Strong's* H3533), which means to tread down, conquer, and subjugate. It means we get to bring the devil into bondage! I think this is glorious news, and a thought we need to keep in the forefront of our minds. We get to take him down instead of him taking us down. We have authority over the confusion and turmoil in our minds. I love how *The Complete Jewish Bible* translates 2 Corinthians 10:4–5:

> *Because the weapons we use to wage war are not worldly. On the contrary, they have God's power for demolishing strongholds. We demolish arguments and every arrogance that raises itself up against the knowledge of God; we take every thought captive and make it obey the Messiah.*   (CJB)

CAST IT DOWN AND OUT

We don't have to fight with worldly weapons. The Holy Spirit will assign spiritual weapons and divine tactics to us through the spirit of revelation. I got free by spending time in the presence of the Lord and partnering with the Holy Spirit. My book *Prophetic Spiritual Warfare* includes information about what the Holy Spirit taught me to conquer spiritual warfare.

When we take a thought captive, we should make it obey the Messiah. In other words, we need to examine the thoughts in our mind and make sure they obey our Lord and align with the Word of God. Any thought that doesn't is stinking thinking, and you need to ditch it and pitch it!

Taking our thoughts captive requires some work on our part. We must make a conscious effort to stay focused, think positive, and cast down any word that does not align with Scripture. When we don't capture our thoughts, they will capture us. It is a choice. If we entertain detrimental thoughts instead of dismissing them, they will take hold of us. We all know practice makes perfect, so how can we practice perfecting our thoughts?

> IF WE ENTERTAIN DETRIMENTAL THOUGHTS INSTEAD OF DISMISSING THEM, THEY WILL TAKE HOLD OF US.

Get adamant and get yourself some holy, righteous anger against the devil! You have a soul, which is your mind, will, and emotions. Use your will, that strong part of you, to be downright ornery and stubborn against any counterproductive thoughts you shouldn't be entertaining.

Discover a practical way that you can identify and cast down thoughts. I have some how-to exercises in my book *Prophetic Spiritual Warfare*, along with tools, visions, and prophetic exercises that brought me out of captivity. One exercise that's helped me is to speak a positive confession out of my mouth when a negative thought comes into my mind. I also lead my mind to think of the truth of what God did in the past in a similar situation. This changes my confession.

The enemy will still try to attack us. Scripture tells us that a subsequent attack will be even worse.

> Then [the unclean spirit] *says, "I will return to my house from which I came." And when it comes, it finds it empty, swept, and put in order. Then it goes and brings with itself seven other spirits more evil than itself, and they enter and dwell there. And the last state of that man is worse than the first.* (Matthew 12:44–45)

Our enemy will never give up because he wants to get us in bondage again. But we know that at the end of the story, he loses.

Release praise during your warfare. Glorify God with your words. Whatever is attacking, release the opposite; be happy, give thanks to God, and release joy. This may sound difficult or impossible, but remember, God is on your side, and nothing is impossible with Him! (See Luke 1:37.) I am not saying to shout at the top of your lungs, "Thank You for this battle," although you should do so if you think it would help. What I'm saying is, "Stay positive." There is much power in hopeful, optimistic thoughts.

RELEASE POSITIVE CHANGE

I grew up in a pessimistic home, so I have given the enemy enough years of my life. I'm changing again and choosing to release positive words against negative situations.

Praise is powerful whether in word or song. Target the following areas to release gratitude:

+ Worship. Put on *"the garment of praise for the spirit of heaviness"* (Isaiah 61:3). Get up and worship. Worship is warfare!

+ Testify of His goodness. Remind yourself of how God intervened in a certain situation, how He either protected you or what you were worried about never came to pass. In one Pennsylvania State University study, researchers learned that 91 percent of the things people worried about never came true.[7] Remember the goodness of God and where He provided, healed, or delivered you.

+ Change your words to praise. Instead of complaining about an ache or pain, speak out and declare, "Thank You, Lord, my body is in perfect working order, and You renew my health." Continue to speak out with positive statements against the negative manifestation you are experiencing.

There is power in our positive confession. The Bible says, *"So then faith comes by hearing, and hearing by the word of God"* (Romans 10:17). Our faith is also increased as we speak out positivity into the atmosphere around us, basing our words on Scripture. We listen to the good, encouraging things we have said, and they come back to us to keep building the positive thoughts in our minds.

POWER AND LOVE OVER FEAR

The second Scripture that has proven to be helpful in my life for releasing mind bondage is this one:

For God has not given us a spirit of fear, but of power and of love and of a sound mind.   (2 Timothy 1:7 NKJV)

People use this Scripture to rebuke and take authority over fear. We release this as a declaration breaking agreement with fear by speaking, "God has not given us (or me) a spirit of fear." We have proclaimed this often in breaking the powers of demonic strongholds, saying and believing that God has not given us a spirit of fear—yet we are still in fear. Why? Because we aren't looking at what He has given us. We didn't break down the full context of this Scripture.

---

7. Lucas S. LaFreniere and Michelle G. Newman, "Exposing Worry's Deceit: Percentage of Untrue Worries in Generalized Anxiety Disorder Treatment," *Behavior Therapy*, July 2020, www.researchgate.net.

The second part of this verse points out that God has given us a spirit of power and love. We know *the greatest of these is love* (1 Corinthians 13:13). Power represents God's authority, so if we have love and power, we can accomplish and conquer anything and everything!

> WE MUST SHIFT OUR THINKING FROM FOCUSING ON THE DEMONIC,
> EVIL SPIRITS AND ATTACKS OF SPIRITUAL WARFARE
> TO THOUGHTS OF LOVE AND POWER.

We are so busy rebuking fear that we aren't receiving what we have, which is God's love and power. Once again, we must shift our thinking from focusing on the demonic, evil spirits and attacks of spiritual warfare to thoughts of love and power! The revelation here should help us renew our minds and rejuvenate our purpose, such as the prophet Elijah experienced. (See 1 Kings 19.)

When we break 2 Timothy 1:7 down in the Greek, we see that the word translated as "fear," *deilós* (*Strong's* G1169), comes from the root word for timidity. It can be intimidation of man or intimidation by the devil, but either way, we have not received a spirit of intimidation. We could read this as, "For God has not given us (or me) a spirit of fear or intimidation."

Intimidation is a blinding spirit that prevents breakthrough because it goes undetected. It hinders us from worshipping freely or prophesying openly. It holds us back from operating in the gifts of the Spirit, declaring audibly with power, or simply praying out loud at a meal surrounded by Christian friends. Intimidation binds us and blocks us. However, most of us have not identified it as a blinding spirit, which means we don't even know it is in operation in our life. Blinding spirits are like that. We are unaware of them.

I once had a blinding spirit of pride. I was a deliverance minister, casting out thousands of demons, but I couldn't see the demon within myself. Yes, you heard that right! I was casting out demons and yet I had one too. But pride, like intimidation, is so blinding that it's difficult to recognize it. For years, two people told me that I had pride, but I could not comprehend it. Then one day, I manifested that demon out. I felt as if blinders had been taken off and I could see for the first time. I am so thankful I had that experience, but not the demon, because now I understand how people can be in denial of their need for deliverance.

SPEAK IT OUT

Years ago, my husband's mom had a mini-stroke and was having a little struggle with clarity of thoughts. Although she was a Christian, she didn't know the power of her words. While she was in the hospital, Ron explained how powerful our words can be and taught her to declare out 2 Timothy 1:7. She quoted this verse repeatedly, and we saw complete transformation in her. She had no other problems with her mind, and the Lord took her home to her heavenly habitation years later.

There is power in Scripture. The Bible says:

> *Then Jesus said to those Jews who believed Him, "If you remain in My word, then you are truly My disciples. You shall know the truth, and the truth shall set you free."*
>
> (John 8:31–32)

This Scripture has two parts. In the first, Jesus said, *"If you remain in My word."* He has given us something to do. We must remain in His Word as a daily choice. We won't know the truth or be set free by it if we aren't in it, understanding it, and speaking it. Remaining in God's Word is not simply reading our Bible, but digging deep into the Word and refusing to get up from studying it until we have learned something. No matter how small of a nugget we find in Scripture, it is still something new that we can apply to our lives.

> REMAINING IN GOD'S WORD IS MORE THAN JUST
> READING THE BIBLE. WE MUST DIG DEEPLY INTO IT AND STUDY IT
> UNTIL WE HAVE LEARNED SOMETHING.

For the second part, we must realize that it isn't truth itself that sets us free. It's the truth we *know* that sets us free. You have to know the Scriptures, revelation, interpretation, and application to be set free.

I look up different translations of Scripture in order to study its full context. Studying this verse, I have referenced three of my favorite versions. We have already read the *New King James Version*, so let's look at how 2 Timothy 1:7 reads in *The Complete Jewish Bible* and *The Holy Bible, Modern English Version* to see what understanding we can gain from the different translations.

+ *For God gave us a Spirit who produces not timidity, but power, love and self-discipline.* (CJB)

+ *For God has not given us the spirit of fear, but of power, and love, and self-control.* (MEV)

The Complete Jewish Bible replaces fear with timidity, which is intimidation, as we noted earlier. Now we need to look at the latter part of the verse, where we are told that God has given us a spirit of self-discipline (CJB) or self-control (MEV). All three of these versions are powerful, telling us we have been given love, power, self-discipline, self-control, and a sound mind! We have a sound mind when we are self-disciplined and practice self-control.

When we have full impartation of this verse, it could read, "God has not given me a spirit of intimidation or fear, but of power, love, self-control, self-discipline, and a sound mind." This power-packed declaration will bring forth liberation when believed and received.

God has given us self-control and self-discipline. Are we too busy *trying* to receive these instead of accepting that we already have them? The Spirit of the living God is inside of us. We can tap into His power anytime we want because Jesus died and left us a Helper, Counselor, Guide, and Friend, the Holy Spirit.

FREEDOM APPLICATION

Every good military commander has a battle plan to win the war. We are in a battle on two fronts: one in our minds and one with demonic forces. Just like a general who gives his soldiers marching orders to carry out and implement his combat plans, so must we order ourselves into battle. Fortunately, we have a great commander-in-chief in the Lord!

In this section, meditate and write out your marching orders on the next page.

MY PLAN OF ACTION TO CONQUER MY MIND BATTLE

1. Identify it: What is the strongest or three most severe mind battles you struggle with?

2. Target it: Is it emotional or spiritual? Is it a work of the flesh, something in your emotions, or do you feel an invisible force pulling you to think negatively and be tormented?

3. Rebuke it: Rebuke means take authority. Like a commander taking authority over his troops, take authority over your emotions or demonic strongholds. Get adamant in your mind, downright stubborn in a good way, that you will not put up with it!

4. Implement it: Make a plan of action. We ruminate when we suffer a mistake or trauma, or are worried about the outcome of an event

5. Attack it: Attach a Scripture that is the opposite of fear or torment. Find scriptural truth to paralyze the thought instead of allowing it to paralyze you.

6. Discover it: What triggers your mind, emotions, feelings, thoughts, fears, depression, or anxiety? If you put a bullet in a gun, nothing happens unless you pull the trigger. What is your mind's trigger? What takes you down the road of destructive thinking?

7. Address it: Address your triggers and targets. How can you avoid them? How can you put up self-protective walls to keep out outside influencers? How can you avoid people, places, or situations that enhance negative thinking and activate the battles within you?

8. Release it: Give it to the Lord. He purchased it at the cross. Cry out to Him and release it to Him. Invite the Holy Spirit to convict and correct you when you are beginning to open yourself up to unnecessary warfare.

Identify it	
Target it	
Rebuke it	
Implement it	
Attack it	
Discover it	
Address it	
Release it	

PROPHETIC ACTIVATION

IDENTIFY THE BATTLE

We all face a battlefield of the mind. You may relate to someone else's battle or have a similar struggle, but only you know the battle you experience. Therefore, the greatest help you can give yourself is journaling out your battle and seeking the Holy Spirit on each step to conquering that particular item.

FORGIVE AND REPENT

Repent for those times you have not trusted the Lord and instead engaged with lying torment. Ask Jesus to forgive you for the times you didn't take your authority. Repent for the times you didn't fight negative thoughts and spoke out words of negativity about your situation.

Pray audibly this prayer of forgiveness:

Jesus, thank You for dying on the cross for me and for the forgiveness of my sins. I repent of wrong actions, of detrimental words I have spoken, negative attitudes, and for not resisting the enemy. I ask You to convict me in the future, Holy Spirit, when attacks try to manifest. Help me arise and fight these attacks with all diligence at the onset, in Jesus's name. Amen!

TARGET THE BATTLE AND BREAK AGREEMENT

Declare and decree:

I break agreement and I command every demonic stronghold in my mind to be evicted in Jesus's name. I speak and decree that I have a sound, self-disciplined, and self-controlled mind. I believe I have the mind of Christ, and my thoughts are focused on good and God. I decree that I capture every thought and submit it to the Word of God. I command every battle in my mind to cease, in Jesus's name.

RELEASE DELIVERANCE

Jesus was in the ministry of deliverance and cast out evil spirits. As you walk out your mind bondage, one of the keys to getting free and staying free is to cast out the correlating spirit that could be manifesting. It could be a spirit of lying, depression, worry, stress, anxiety, fear, mind-binding, or torment. Pray audibly and command the spirit to leave: "Spirit of _____, I cast you out, in Jesus's name."

WARFARE PRAYER DECLARATIONS

+ I diffuse and break up every tormenting thought. I control my thoughts; they don't control me!

+ I demolish every stronghold in my thought life and command my thoughts to align with the Word of God.

+ I interrupt the enemy's plans to steal, kill, and destroy my thinking and God's mission for my life.

+ I interrupt every assignment against my mind and reverse every direct warfare order against me.

+ I annihilate every high power and principality targeting my mind, in Jesus's name.

REMOVE THE BATTLE

Removing the battle takes effort. There is no room for passivity, procrastination, or stagnancy. You can't get stuck thinking that you are destined to live in defeat. Conquering every mind battle comes from consistently casting it down. You have to fight. Find a way to set a goal where you can focus and be determined to persevere even when the battle isn't as intense as usual. Be consistent in the fight.

PROPHETIC APPLICATION

1. Develop a plan for taking your thoughts captive. What concrete strategies can you put in place?

2. Try studying the Bible in a different way or with different translations to bring forth new revelation. Instead of quantity reading, seek quality studying. Write new word meanings in your Bible to better understand the Scripture.

FREEDOM THOUGHT

Your mind is valuable artillery for the kingdom of God. Protect it with all diligence.

7

EXPOSING MIND-BINDING SPIRITS

For years, my mind was plagued by evil spirits that prevented me from redirecting my thoughts. It was not constant torment, but appeared during specific circumstances that caused fear, stress, and worry. I could feel the anguish in my mind, pulling me strongly toward the very thing afflicting me. My mind was like a piece of steel drawn irresistibly to a magnet of negative thinking. I could not pull away from what I was feeling. An invisible force was locking me down, paralyzing my thoughts. I was a Spirit-filled, tongue-talking Christian who cast demons out of people...and yet I felt the devil torment my mind.

I tried to pray, worship, and read my Bible. I attempted to refocus my thoughts. I would get up and get busy. I would do everything in the natural I knew how to do, but I couldn't escape the mind-binding spirits that would lure me into focusing on fear. I had to fight this battle alone because no one understood my struggle. They could not relate to it, nor comprehend what I was going through. I could be tormented for hours at a time until my mind broke free.

I'm not sure how it happened. I didn't have the tools to break the mind battle. The only thing I can tell you is that I began to seek the Holy Spirit. I didn't know of any books on mind-binding spirits; I had never even heard of them until the Holy Spirit gave me the revelation.

HOW A MIND-BINDING SPIRIT OPERATES

Mind-binding spirits draw and lure you into the same way of thinking from which you are trying to escape. They seductively draw your thoughts away from good and God to negativity, fear, anxiety, sin, trauma, and lies. Mind-binding spirits are blinding; you don't see that you are in bondage to a demonic spirit. Instead, it is misidentified as a vain imagination or the idea that you can't control your thoughts. Identifying and exposing mind-binding spirits, as we are now, will help you to be free of them. You can't conquer and cast out what you don't know is in operation.

> MIND-BINDING SPIRITS SEDUCTIVELY DRAW YOUR THOUGHTS AWAY FROM GOOD AND GOD TO NEGATIVITY, FEAR, ANXIETY, SIN, TRAUMA, AND LIES.

Mind-binding spirits try to steal your destiny, prevent your freedom, and keep you in sin and bondage. As your mind is locked down and stuck in a particular direction, feelings and false realities can invade your soul and make you feel as if you cannot live in your full potential.

MIND BATTLES

When we struggle with an emotional ailment and cannot get freedom after years of effort, we need to explore the concept that something greater than our emotions is behind the battle. Think of rejection, fear, worry, unworthiness, or condemnation. People usually wrestle with these things for twenty or thirty years. The problem has followed them throughout their lives. They have tried to get freedom and obtain victory; they have studied books and sought counseling. There has to be an aspect we missed because our minds are neuroplastic, meaning they can change, so why can't we stop some thoughts or torments?

What stronghold you have struggled with in your mind? Rejection, fear, worry, unworthiness, or condemnation? Have you ever explored reasons why you can't break free from it?

A mind-binding spirit keeps you in torment of fear, believing the lie of rejection, constantly worrying, not accepting your worth, or feeling defeated with condemnation. This demonic spirit needs to be identified and cast out of your soul.

DEFINING MIND BINDING

Emotional battles can be separated into two categories: our flesh and natural battles; and an evil, mind-binding spirit. How do you identify the difference when you have suffered for so long? Here are some key symptoms of a mind-binding spirit:

+ Confusion – This is the evil work of the enemy. (See James 3:16.) When you experience repeated confusion, you become indecisive.

+ Torment – Your mind feels out of control. As it is tormented and locked down, you are unable to get out of a paralysis state to redirect and refocus your thoughts.

+ Fear – You are afraid of making the wrong decision or not making the right decision, or fear manifests in your situation, making you afraid of what is happening.

+ Emotional turmoil – You waver back and forth, unable to make up your mind. You don't understand why you feel this way. You truly know better but don't know how to pull yourself toward a good and God direction.

> AMONG THE KEY SYMPTOMS OF A MIND-BINDING SPIRIT ARE CONFUSION, TORMENT, FEAR, AND EMOTIONAL TURMOIL.

Unless you know someone who has experienced something similar, no one will understand your mind battle except you. I wish

I could talk it out with you and everyone else reading this book, but that's simply not possible. However, I do believe that once you have finished reading this book and completed the exercises, you will be on your way to freedom.

To discover your mind battle, you need to determine what is fueling it. In this exercise, write down your fear, torment, lie, worry, and trauma beside each circle. Identify your feelings and think about each one to discover the ultimate root to your battle.

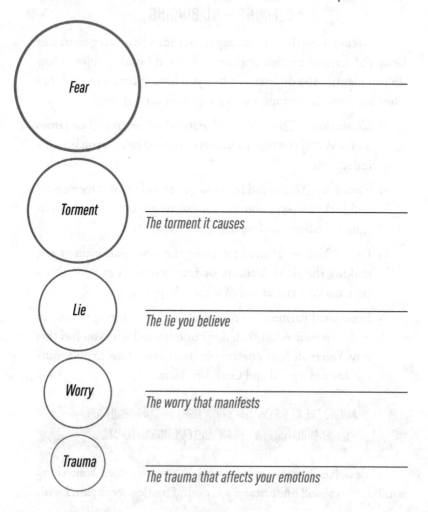

Fear _____

Torment _____
The torment it causes

Lie _____
The lie you believe

Worry _____
The worry that manifests

Trauma _____
The trauma that affects your emotions

SIN BATTLES

One of the operations of mind-binding spirits is to keep people in a place of repeated sin. For instance, someone who has tried to give up pornography or masturbation may be drawn and lured back into the sin. I'm using sexual immorality here as an example, but this applies to all sin and battles.

If you have a sin from which you have repented and you truly do want to change, but you never seem to gain complete victory over the sin, you are dealing with a mind-binding spirit. The entire battle isn't being exposed, so it can't be released. When you seek deliverance from sin, after repenting, seeking the Lord for forgiveness, and forgiving yourself, a continued issue in the spiritual realm still needs to be addressed.

The ministry of deliverance includes casting out demons as Jesus modeled in the Gospels. In the case of sexual immorality, to get freedom from the demonic spirits that are attacking, we must cast out spirits of lust, perversion, sexual immorality, unclean spirits, and other defiling spirits. We fall short and don't receive complete freedom because we need to cast out the evil spirits and break agreement with the sin. This will release the sin in the natural and the hold we experience in the spiritual. Breaking agreement proclaims we are making a decision not to participate in unclean acts.

BINDING STRONGMAN SPIRITS

In the demonic hierarchy, there are strongman spirits we need to address. Jesus talked about the strongman:

> Or else how can one enter a strong man's house and plunder his goods unless he first binds the strong man? And then he will plunder his house.   (Matthew 12:29)

Unless we bind and restrict the strongman and sweep our house clean, we are brought back into bondage again—this time, more severe than the first.

> *When an unclean spirit goes out of a man, it passes through dry places seeking rest, but finds none. Then it says, "I will return to my house from which I came." And when it comes, it finds it empty, swept, and put in order. Then it goes and brings with itself seven other spirits more evil than itself, and they enter and dwell there. And the last state of that man is worse than the first. So shall it be also with this evil generation.*
> (Matthew 12:43–45)

It is a three-part process: binding the strongman; casting out the spirit; and renewing our thoughts.

Mind-binding spirits are strongmen that need to be cast out. When we look at Jesus's ministry, He didn't simply say to these evil spirits, "Leave this person alone," or "Stop bothering them." He took authority over the demon and cast it out with authority. Jesus gave us the full authority over the strongman, so we can cast it out just as He did. (See Mark 16:17; Matthew 10:8.) He gave us authority over all things. (See Luke 10:19; 9:1.) We must take that authority over the strongman.

One of the characteristics of this spirit is that it is indeed mind-blinding. You may not realize that you have it. Whether it attacks you with fear, depression, rejection, or sexual immorality, you must get intentional about removing it. Your prayer life must be intense so that you can cast out the mind-binding spirit and stop the repeated cycle of sin.

Deliverance is a continuing process that involves resisting temptation, no longer sinning, repenting, and changing. We must guard our minds because sometimes, a mind-binding spirit will attack again. Unfortunately, whether we fail to capture a negative tormenting thought or are being drawn and lured into sin, we are human, so we will miss the mark and mess up again.

> **WHEN AN EVIL SPIRIT HAS BEEN HARASSING YOU FOR TWENTY YEARS, YOU CAN'T EXPECT TO GET FREE AND STAY FREE IN TWENTY MINUTES.**

When an evil spirit has been harassing you for twenty years, you can't expect to get free and stay free in twenty minutes. It is a walking-out process and could take years for you to receive complete freedom. During that time, you need healing and equipping so that you learn how to fight and resist the enemy. Inner healing is vital in order for you to receive your deliverance.

While trying to obtain freedom, you may become discouraged and lose some ground, but two years is often the length of time it takes to unlearn twenty years' worth of coping skills, mind habits, and lack of perseverance. You probably want twenty years' worth of oppression reversed in twenty days, but I have repeatedly witnessed it taking two years because the enemy will not give up in his attempt to lure you into sin or draw you into wrong thinking. Still, you will have obtained the tools *"to extinguish all the fiery arrows of the evil one"* (Ephesians 6:16). By taking your authority, subsequent attacks will be easier and faster to master.

Sin and mind battles can be driven by thoughts we ruminate. Rumination is our minds continually circling back to the same thought. We can control our thoughts and what we choose to think about repeatedly. We can either contemplate our problem and systematically come up with a solution, or become overly fixated with the situation and ensnared in mental bondage.

Mind-binding spirits are similar to rumination, but they come from the spiritual realm. They pressure us to stay focused in one direction, drawing us toward an addiction, sin, torment, or emotional bondage. Since they are demonic spirits, unlike rumination, it is not as easy to turn our thoughts toward good and God. We have to fight the demonic spirit and resist the torment. We have to conquer it in the natural, emotional, and spiritual spheres. Conquering it takes a conscious effort to fight and resist the torment and demonic draw. We have to engage naturally by getting our bodies involved. We cannot merely sit and allow the torment to play out. Getting active by standing while praying, for example, is one way to become physically involved.

You have to emotionally engage in the battle and fight the stress, anxiety, worry, and fear. You can't allow yourself to go into a depressive state of mind. You need to capture and cast down the thought constantly. Spiritually, you need to fight. Resist and take authority over your flesh. If it wants you to stay in a dark room with the blinds shut, you have to say, "No, I will get up and go for a walk." You have to do what your flesh doesn't want to do. You can't cave in.

We are a three-part being, as I discuss in chapter ten, and our spirit should rule over our flesh. The Lord revealed to me the power of submitting my flesh to my spirit when I was on a solitude retreat with Him. It was windy and forty degrees outside, but He told me to go out and pray on a cliff overlooking the waters of Lake Michigan. It was a prophetic action to learn how to submit my flesh. I had to stay out there and pray audibly until the Spirit of the Lord released me. To win the war that rages in our minds, we must engage our entire three-part being. It is never just a spiritual warfare battle.

ONE WAY TO VICTORY

Before sending soldiers off to war, the military trains them emotionally and physically. Besides being mentally prepared for their mission, troops must be physically fit, capable of carrying a heavy load, and able to shoot a rifle with precision accuracy to hit their target. It is the same with us when we engage in a war. We need to be all-in, or we will be targeted and devoured by our enemy.

People cannot win the war in their minds if they feel defeated or get tired of fighting. I'm personally very thankful for the military that they don't give up fighting on our behalf when they are fatigued but keep their eyes focused on their mission.

You have a task to accomplish in the kingdom of God, a mission and a purpose to which He has called you. You need to have the discipline to press through to your breakthrough.

When mind-binding spirits are attacking you, you may be in the greatest battle of your life. You will never win it if you don't fight. You need to pray when you don't feel like praying and fight when you are being tormented. Reach out to some people and ask them to help you pray through the struggle.

I remember being pierced with torment when I had an adverse reaction to an over-the-counter medication. The enemy was torturing my mind, making me think the worst would happen. I grabbed my husband and asked him to sit on the couch and help me pray the torment away. I was healed and delivered after we had prayed for one and a half hours. In other instances, I have texted a friend to have someone pray with me to expose the enemy and break free from the torment I was experiencing. Although I asked for help, *I* had to pray. I first had to take my authority. I couldn't leave it up to my friends or husband to pray for me through the battle. It was my battle to fight, not theirs.

I believe this is where Christians don't engage in the battle enough. We are too quick to call a prayer line, enlist a friend, post on social media, or whine and complain to our ministry leader. We want everyone else to fight the battle for us because we are being tormented. But it is *our* battle. When we engage in the fight, we conquer the victimhood and defeatism that the enemy wants to use to bind us. We were made to fight. We are warriors, not worriers. We are victorious, not victims. We must fight.

I have waged so many wars, but I have also lost so many special moments because the enemy pierced my mind. He still tries to do these things, but now I know how to pull my thoughts back toward good and God.

> WHEN FACED WITH MIND-BINDING SPIRITS, IT IS OUR BATTLE.
> WE WERE MADE TO FIGHT. WE ARE WARRIORS, NOT WORRIERS.
> WE ARE VICTORIOUS, NOT VICTIMS.

The idea that our minds are being bound is the core of this book.

You have tried to receive freedom, but you are reading this book because you still haven't received the freedom you desire. Therefore, it is time to consider that a greater force can be at work behind your mind bondage, an unseen, invisible force called a demonic spirit.

FREEDOM APPLICATION

I have a saying, "If in doubt, cast it out." If you don't know whether you have a demonic spirit or a flesh problem, try casting out the demonic spirit. It only takes a minute of your time and a few sentences. If your mind then feels better, you are on your way to greater freedom. If you don't feel anything happen, you've wasted nothing except a minutes of your time. If in doubt, cast it out. Let's do it now. Declare:

I break agreement with every mind-binding spirit. I command every tormenting demon to get out of me in Jesus's name. Mind-binding spirit, get out in the name of Jesus. I speak and decree that I am set free of all mind torment by the blood of Jesus.

PROPHETIC ACTIVATION

IDENTIFY THE BATTLE

What feelings arise within you during your battle? As discussed in this chapter, can you pull yourself out of the emotional turmoil, or do you feel like something has just taken over your emotions? There is no shame in discovering a demonic spirit may be oppressing you. There is freedom in knowing the truth. Spend time praying, fasting, and seeking the Holy Spirit for revelatory truth about your situation.

FORGIVE AND REPENT

We can be weighed down with guilt, shame, condemnation, and regret when dealing with mind bondages. These are emotions that we need to release and we may need to forgive ourselves for manifesting. Forgiving ourselves can be the hardest part, but let's do it now. Pray this prayer of forgiveness:

> Lord Jesus, I confess to You that I forgive myself for any feelings that do not properly align with my situation and what the Word of God says about me. I proclaim at this moment that I forgive myself. I repeat, I forgive myself, I forgive myself…In Jesus's name, amen!

It can be difficult to say, "I forgive myself," but just keep doing it and repeating it or return to it until you receive trust and peace.

TARGET THE BATTLE AND BREAK AGREEMENT

> I break agreement and annihilate every mind-binding spirit in my life. I cast down and destroy the torment these spirits cause and the turmoil that manifests. In the name of Jesus, I speak and decree I am set free from every mind-binding torment and I command mind-binding spirits to deactivate and stop attacking me. I proclaim

that my liberation is here. I command every mind-binding spirit to get out of my soul, in Jesus's name.

RELEASE DELIVERANCE

Jesus was in the ministry of deliverance and cast out evil spirits. You are walking out your mind bondage now. One of the keys to getting free and staying free is to cast out the correlating spirit that could be manifesting. Pray audibly and command the spirt to leave. It could be a spirit of lying, depression, worry, stress, anxiety, fear, mind-binding, or torment. Declare: "Spirit of _____, I cast you out, in Jesus's name."

WARFARE PRAYER DECLARATIONS

+ I bind and cast out every tormenting evil spirit in the name of Jesus.

+ I rebuke and cut off every defiling spirit that would attack my thought life, in Jesus's name.

+ I destroy and break up anything I have done in the natural to cause these attacks in the spiritual.

+ I command and decree every mind-binding spirit to release its hold on me and get out, in Jesus's name.

+ I annihilate with the fire of God every principality and evil power assigned to attack my mind and command them to leave me, in Jesus's name.

REMOVE THE BATTLE

Victimhood and defeatist mentalities are detrimental in our walk with the Lord and our fight against the enemy. Often we've been so wounded that we don't know how to pull our minds out of negativity. Our minds need to be renewed to recognize who we are in Christ and that where we are seated leads to victory, not defeat.

Where do you need to remove the battle in your mind and see yourself differently to live differently?

PROPHETIC APPLICATION

1. What practical thing can you do in the natural when mind-binding torment attacks you?

2. Establish an accountability system of friends and family members to assist you through torment.

FREEDOM THOUGHT

Torment can't exist if you resist.

8

EXPOSING FEAR'S HIDDEN FORCE

During storms when I was a kid, we would go into the crawl space—basically a hole in the floor. My mom would always try to protect us and make sure we didn't get hurt. Storms in Michigan weren't that bad, but we would "batten down the hatches," as she would say. Unfortunately, I carried that into my adulthood, not as a protective mechanism but as fear penetrating to the very core of my being. When storms came, I would snuggle up in my husband's arms. I needed to feel safe and protected. Our daughters were also fearful of storms while growing up. I'm not proud to say that I taught them that behavior. Fear triggered in me and caused an emotional response and natural reaction. My mother's words would cycle back in my mind. I couldn't break free because even when I was an adult, she would call and tell me strong winds or severe weather was heading my way.

I was praying and discerning while writing this book, and the revelation that poured out was astonishing. The Holy Spirit revealed that control is a driving force behind fear in some people. I first looked at my own life, having been bound to fear for so many years, and I didn't see where the fear and control correlated, but then my daughter said something about fear, and my husband came home from work with a revelation. Everything the Holy Spirit had been showing me started to come together.

I'm sure I could arrive at many topics in which fear and control collide, but since the Holy Spirit revealed storms and people's fears of them to me, I would like to set some of those captives free with this chapter. Even though we discuss physical storms in this context, I believe the principles could also be applied to the storms we face in life.

FEAR IN THE STORM

Jesus knew a little bit about storms. He was in a boat with His disciples when a storm arose on the water. Both the wind and the sea were raging. Of course, Jesus didn't fear. He controlled the storm instead of the storm or fear controlling Him. He wasn't afraid that the storm would cause damage or death. He was at peace. One definition of *peace* from *Merriam-Webster's Dictionary* is "freedom from disquieting or oppressive thoughts or emotions." To be "at peace," it says, means "in a state of concord or tranquility."

> WHEN WE HAVE PEACE LIKE JESUS,
> WE HAVE FREEDOM FROM DISTURBANCE, FEAR, CONTROL, ANXIETY,
> OR ANY UNHEALTHY EMOTION.

When we have *shalom* (peace) like Jesus, we have freedom from disturbance, fear, control, anxiety, or any unhealthy emotion. Just defining the word peace brings forth deliverance. We can declare the interpretation of this as, "By having peace and trusting Jesus, I have freedom from disturbing, oppressive, and mind-binding torment."

Let's break down the storm from the Gospel of Mark:

That same day, when the evening came, He said to them, "Let us go cross to the other side." When they had sent the crowd away, they took Him in the boat just as He was. There were also other little boats with Him. A great wind storm arose,

and the waves splashed into the boat, so that it was now fill-
ing the boat. He was in the stern asleep on a pillow. They
woke Him and said, "Teacher, do You not care that we are
perishing?" He rose and rebuked the wind, and said to the
sea, "Peace, be still!" Then the wind ceased and there was a
great calm. He said to them, "Why are you so fearful? How
is that you have no faith?" They feared greatly and said to one
another, "What kind of Man is He, that even the wind and
the sea obey Him?"   (Mark 4:35–41)

Jesus was at peace, asleep on a pillow. The disciples awoke Him
and said, *"Teacher, do You not care that we are perishing?"* Jesus, still
in peace, *"rebuked the wind, and said to the sea, 'Peace, be still!'"* The
disciples were freaking out. Jesus confirms this by saying to them,
"Why are you so fearful?" He goes on to relate this to a lack of faith
on their part.

Here we see a storm raging unabated. The disciples can't control what is happening, and they are in fear. Do you see the correlation here? The disciples were in fear because they couldn't control
the storm. They couldn't take authority over it, so they were afraid
for their lives.

FEAR AND CONTROL IN PEOPLE

My daughter has been walking through the deliverance process of fear. She prays about most decisions, has a reverential
fear of the Lord, and wants to be obedient to Him. However, she
sometimes can get confused when trying to discern if she should
do something or not. In our conversations, while helping her to
receive freedom, it became apparent that the core of her issue, the
source of the confusion, was fear. She has felt fear because if she
makes the wrong decision, she or one of her family members may
get hurt. When I asked her the root cause of the turmoil about
making the wrong decision, she said, "I can't control it." When we

further diagrammed the process backward to discover the root, it was clear that the issue is more control and torment than fear. Control is a hidden component and driving force behind fear.

Knowing I was doing this research, my husband came home one day and said, "Honey, you have got to hear this. I have some revelation for your book." Ron personally loves storms, but he had been talking to a coworker who hates them. Why? "Because I can't control them" was the reply.

Reflecting back on my childhood, I see that although my mom was protective and fear was the root cause of her behavior, she was trying to control the situation. She felt a lack of control that manifested as fear. Therefore, to get free from mind battles, we must discover not only what is identified easily in our conscious, but also what is the root cause or driving force in our subconscious.

> TO GET FREE FROM MIND BATTLES, WE MUST DISCOVER NOT ONLY WHAT IS IDENTIFIED EASILY IN OUR CONSCIOUS, BUT ALSO THE DRIVING FORCE IN OUR SUBCONSCIOUS.

FREEDOM APPLICATION

Mother wounds are a common area in which we can suffer mind battles due to control. However, not all control is from our parents; some of it we have put on ourselves. In this exercise, identify the following:

FIRST EXERCISE

Discover how you have been controlled. You see "control" written in the top circle. In the other circles, write the ways in which you have been controlled so you can see how they connect. For example, you could have been controlled by words, appearance, friends, actions, homework expectations, or chores. Think of how and when you were controlled as a child that affected you.

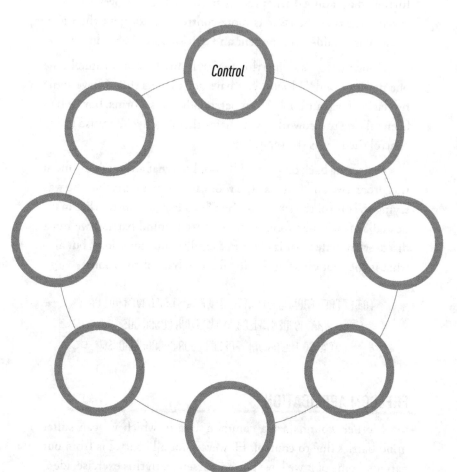

SECOND EXERCISE

Discover how control manifests out of you. On the next page, write in the circles how you control things or situations. Examples could include eating, money, time, ideas, spoken words, getting my own way, protection, etc.

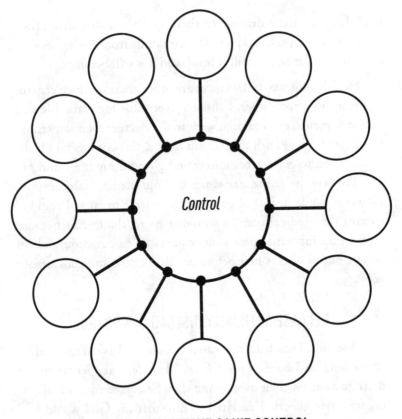

WE FEAR WHAT WE CAN'T CONTROL

Lack of control makes us seek to control and attributes to fear. Control and fear are both mind bondages. I was controlling early on in my marriage. I wanted to control where our group of friends went out to eat and which side of the family we would visit over the holidays. It produced mind bondage because I had to think of ways to manipulate to get my way. I would be under stress and worry about getting my way. Bondage is bondage. It just manifests differently.

Control and fear can manifest in driving a car. Some people insist on driving no matter if it's the husband's vehicle or the wife's because they have to be in control. They feel out of control and fearful if they aren't driving. In their opinion, if they drive, they can protect everyone and prevent their family from having an accident. It is still fear, it is still control, and it is still bondage.

Health ailments and finances are other areas in which control and fear drive each other. I suffered from this for years. I feared health ailments, but I seldom went to the doctor when something manifested. I had faith for *Jehovah Rapha*, the Lord Who Heals. I want God to get the testimony and glory in my life—and He has. I've been healed fifteen times without medical intervention. However, I was in fear of going to the doctor because I couldn't control the medical costs. I wouldn't go to the doctor because we have an insurance plan that requires us to pay thousands of dollars out of pocket first before our deductible and coinsurance activates.

RELEASE AUTHORITY INSTEAD OF CONTROL

One time, I needed a root canal and crown. I asked the dentist, "How long do I have to get it fixed?" He told me, "These things don't go away on their own"—and then he cursed me with all the negative side effects. I declared to him that my God would heal me. I claimed, prayed, and received prayer several times and didn't go back to the dentist for six months. When I went back, he told me the problem was still there, the tooth was still abscessed, but I knew I had been healed because I wasn't feeling the same manifestations in my mouth that I had been. I went home and prayed; the Lord told me to go to a surgeon. The surgeon ran a series of tests and said I didn't need a root canal. Praise God! I did get healed!

I couldn't control my situation in the natural for the root canal I needed or the cost I would incur, but I *could* control the situation by taking my authority in Jesus Christ. Jesus died and gave us authority. When we use that authority, we can expect spiritual and natural results. Authority trumps fear!

People who fear accidents and need to drive a car to have control need to take their authority over that vehicle. My daughter doesn't have that problem. She prays protection audibly whenever she gets in her truck or my car. She'll say, "Who's going to pray?" As we back up in the driveway or head down the road, we take authority over the vehicle, command no accidents or breakdowns, and plead the blood of Jesus.

It is the same with storms. Jesus spoke to the storm and rebuked the wind, taking authority over it. He stilled the waters of the sea. He kept His perfect peace and released authority. Therefore, protection came forth, the storm ceased, and no one was hurt.

We have that same authority. My husband and I have taken it many times over storms, wind, hurricanes, and tornados. We take authority and our property, vehicles, and animals are spared.

I used to fear storms so much that I only felt safe in my husband's arms. I sought my husband for protection rather than my heavenly Father. Once I learned that my Father is my protector (see Psalm 91), I didn't have to fear, and my faith increased. Even though I like to snuggle with my husband, I no longer need to do it out of fear.

When storms come our way, I know God is going to protect us. We walk around our house, inside or out, depending on the conditions, and decree, declare, and take authority. I don't fear because I have faith that when I speak, my words are prophetically assigned and targeted to get results. I don't fear because I have seen God's hand of protection. I serve a loving Father who is my protector, and He has given me the authority over all things.

Authority is similar to control, but they are not the same. The dictionary defines *control* as "to exercise restraining or directing influence over; to have power over; to reduce the incidence or severity of especially to innocuous levels." *Authority*, on the other hand, is "power to influence or command thought, opinion, or behavior." As we see in the Bible, we have the authority to influence, direct, and restrain. Instead of desiring to control a situation, we need to take authority over it. Jesus gave us the authority to command storms, evict demons, and speak to sickness and tell it to go. When we know the authority that Jesus has given us, we have no reason to fear.

> WE MAY NOT BE ABLE TO CONTROL THINGS THAT HAPPEN TO US, BUT WE CAN TAKE AUTHORITY OVER THEM.

If we want to get rid of fear and mind battles, we must know our authority. We may not be able to control things that happen to us, but we can take authority over them after they occur or while we are being attacked. Authority comes from taking action and speaking out about our situation. We bind and restrict negative things from happening, call forth the heavens to open on our behalf, and release every perfect thing.

Authority comes by knowing who we are in Christ and knowing fear does not have to rule in our hearts. It is living out Psalm 91 daily that God will protect us when we are in the secret place. It is submitting to the lordship of Jesus, humbling ourselves before the Father, and allowing Him to be our protector so we can lay down the need to control.

We can try to control situations, but in the long run, we won't prevail. We are in the end times, and many things will be out of control. We should learn now that God is our protector. We must evict fear and walk in faith. We are coming to a critical point where we need to trust like never before if we want to be in peace. Faith is the opposite of fear. Faith and trust are interchangeable. Trust and peace correlate. When we trust, we will have peace.

FREEDOM APPLICATION

Authority is a vital element of walking out of mind bondage. You have the right to command those tormenting thoughts to go. You must arise, take your authority, speak to those tormenting thoughts, and command them to leave. Break agreement with control and fear. Say, "I release control and fear from my life, in Jesus's name. Get out of me!"

Every time a plaguing thought comes to torment, you take authority. Speak out loud, "Get out and go, in Jesus's name." Keep doing it until you have victory. Jesus died so you could have authority over all things. One of those things is your mind. Take authority over it before the thoughts take authority over you and prevent natural, spiritual, and emotional movement.

You can do it! Do it now!

PROPHETIC ACTIVATION

IDENTIFY THE BATTLE

Look at the fear, worry, and stress in your life. Where do you feel you aren't in control? When you look at control, do you see characteristics from your parents that you could be manifesting? Trauma and abuse can also lead to the desire to be in control. What needs to be rooted out of your past to walk free from mind battles?

FORGIVE AND REPENT

When we desire control, rather than submitting to God's will, it is rebellion. The Bible says, *"Rebellion is as the sin of witchcraft"* (1 Samuel 15:23). When we rebel, we are saying we don't trust God with our lives. By releasing repentance, we can turn things around and give up our desire for control. Pray this prayer audibly:

Father God, I release control from my life. Father God, I ask You to forgive me for areas in which I want to be in control. I will trust You. I know You are my protector. I forgive myself for desiring to be in control. I repent of taking actions in my own strength instead of in the strength of the Lord.

TARGET THE BATTLE AND BREAK AGREEMENT

I break agreement with control, rebellion, fear, stress, anxiety, and worry. I command all control to leave me. When I am weary, I will trust in the Lord. When I am fearful and need a protector, I know He will be my provider. God loves me and He is a shield and fortress around me. I will draw strength from the Lord that only He can provide. I choose this day to release control.

RELEASE DELIVERANCE

Jesus was in the ministry of deliverance and cast out evil spirits. You are walking out your mind bondage now. One of the keys to getting free and staying free is to cast out the correlating spirit that could be manifesting. Pray audibly and command any of the following spirits to leave: lying, depression, worry, stress, anxiety, fear, mind-binding, torment, unforgiveness, and offense. Declare, "Spirit of _____, I cast you out, in Jesus's name."

WARFARE PRAYER DECLARATIONS

- I bind and rebuke a spirit of control from activating in my life. I proclaim I yield to the Holy Spirit.
- I repent and renounce every need to control. I remove any entitlements and wrong thought patterns that lead to control.
- I command that my emotions are pliable and malleable, that I am not stubborn and unchangeable.

+ I trust my heavenly Father is my protector, the one who orchestrates my steps and leads and guides me in my ways.

+ I remove wrong mindsets and soul ties to my parents that may have bound me with a spirit of control.

REMOVE THE BATTLE

Control can be so subtle that we miss it. We often compare controlling people to Jezebel in the Bible (see 1 Kings 21), but there are different degrees of control. We all have a level of control, things we like to control, and ways we want to be in control. We must honestly seek inside ourselves for areas that can bring forth true freedom, even if we might not be proud of them. Ask the Holy Spirit to convict and correct you in areas of your life where you need to relinquish control.

PROPHETIC APPLICATION

+ Where have you been controlled in your life?

+ How can you submit to the Lord and lay down the control? Is there a root of control from which you need healing?

FREEDOM THOUGHT

Besides our spiritual walk and our actions, there is nothing and no one we can truly control.

9

TRUST RELEASES BREAKTHROUGH

I have experienced multiple trust journeys, so finding just one to open this chapter is difficult. However, I would like to point out two things before we dive in:

1. Behind every mind battle is a place in our lives where we don't trust the Lord.

2. Every trust journey the Lord has called me to has been worth it.

The realization that I was not trusting God was almost too overwhelming to bear. I love the Lord with everything in me. I am a worshipper to the core of my being. My lack of trust didn't make sense—and yet it was true. One day as I was walking and worshipping to spend time with God, He revealed to me that I didn't trust Him. I was singing a hymn at the top of my lungs when one sentence I belted out gripped and pierced me to the core of my being. I knew it was a conviction from the Holy Spirit, and the revelation grieved me. I was truly in a season of hot pursuit of God, so the thought that I didn't trust Him crushed me.

As I proceeded forward in my trust journey, I learned that many Christians—perhaps all of us—have a trust issue. The thought that we don't trust our heavenly Father is a little hard to comprehend when we need trust in order to follow Christ. It requires a self-evaluation to determine what trusting and not trusting mean. It takes a moment to digest the information and consider that maybe we do not trust the Lord.

We are trying to get free of fear in this book. Fear is the opposite of faith. Faith and trust are interchangeable. When we read Scripture verses on faith, adding the word "trust" makes them more revelatory and personal. *The Complete Jewish Bible* uses the word *trust* for *faith* several times, which gives Scripture a deeper context.

PROPHETIC ACTION LEADS TO TRUST

There is a natural and spiritual correlation between the Bible and the world in which we live. What happens in the natural shifts something in the spiritual, and what happens in the spiritual releases something in the natural. The Bible teaches the principles of binding and loosing.

> *Yes! I tell you people that whatever you prohibit on earth will be prohibited in heaven, and whatever you permit on earth will be permitted in heaven. To repeat, I tell you that if two of you here on earth agree about anything people ask, it will be for them from my Father in heaven.*
>
> (Matthew 18:18–19 cjb)

Our greatest victories in trust and breaking fear come from performing prophetic actions. These are movements or assignments that we accomplish when led by the Holy Spirit.

Early in my walk with the Lord, I was trying to break through the veil and get into a place of intimacy with Him. As I worshipped, He told me to take a couple of steps forward in the natural as a prophetic action to enter His presence. Another time, He required me to take an entirely different prophetic action as I tried to get a breakthrough from fear. It was snowing outside, and I was raised not to drive on snowy roads. As I was lying prostrate before the Lord that day, He told me to get up, go to the store, and purchase a sign that read, "Freedom." I obtained freedom that day as I drove in the snow.

If God calls you to take a natural action as an act of deliverance, do it without hesitation.

OBEDIENCE VS. CONTROL

The Lord requires obedience. It brings pleasure to His heart as we make obedience an act of worship. Being both obedient and disciplined will break the bondage that has manifested for years. God isn't just seeking us to be obedient and *eventually* do what He calls us to do; He requires us to act upon His instructions immediately, with discipline. We shouldn't need Him to repeatedly convict us in order to act.

> GOD ISN'T JUST SEEKING US TO BE OBEDIENT AND
> EVENTUALLY DO WHAT HE CALLS US TO DO;
> HE REQUIRES US TO ACT UPON HIS INSTRUCTIONS IMMEDIATELY.

We don't always act on the Holy Spirit's instructions because we desire control. We want to control our money, our time, and our health decisions. We don't want to be told what to do. People are often in bondage to fear and control simultaneously. (See chapter eight.) One of the ways we can gauge whether we are bound to control is determining whether we trust Him for what He is calling us to do. Let's do the following prophetic exercise right now.

FREEDOM APPLICATION

+ How long does it usually take you to respond when the Holy Spirit calls you to do something?

+ What causes the delay, or why do you delay?

- What instructions are you still waiting to complete that He has given to you?
- What is preventing you from activating those instructions?

HOW WE DON'T TRUST GOD

There are different areas in our lives where we don't trust God. In this section, I will discuss some of the main ways we don't respond to God in trust, the driving force behind our lack of trust, and what we are missing in our lives as a result.

RELATIONAL

We all have an imperfect human nature. Others may reject us for reasons we do not understand, making us suffer emotional wounds that become obstacles and barriers that keep us locked down and self-protecting. As human beings, we desire friendship, love, and relationships. When we don't seek our inner healing and freedom from mind bondage, we can and will hurt other people. Hurt brings in feelings of unforgiveness and bitterness. When a relationship has gone bad, we often feel offended, betrayed, and rejected.

> WHEN WE ARE REPEATEDLY REJECTED,
> WE DEVELOP A FEAR OF REJECTION, SO WE PUT UP PROTECTIVE
> WALLS AND BARRICADES IN OUR MINDS.

As a deliverance minister, I believe 80 percent of Christians have had rejection as a stronghold in their lives, but the other 20 percent can relate to it somehow. When friends reject us repeatedly, we develop a fear of rejection. We put up protective walls and barricades in our minds because we're afraid of being rejected again by friends, spouses, ministry leaders, or employers. Familiar spirits attack us and create the same cycles of rejection, binding us to fear. All of this comes from believing others' lies and overcompensating by being a people-pleaser.

Behind rejection is a fear that you won't have friends; behind the fear is the lie that you believe that no one will treat you fairly or love you for who you are. Behind the lie is a place where you aren't trusting God—in this case, you aren't trusting Him for good, quality friendships, or for Him to be your ultimate friend and all you need.

When we fear being rejected again, we believe a lie that triggers fear, which ultimately leads to a place in our minds and hearts where we don't trust our heavenly Father.

BLINDING SPIRITS

Emotional ailments all have triggers. Stress, anxiety, depression, and worry are all triggered by fear. You get depressed because there is something you are worried or fearful about. Behind that fear is a lie or untruth that has been activated in your mind and appears as a reality. It is a blinding spirit. You believe the lie, and you can't decipher the difference between that and the truth.

This is one reason why people stay in a place of bondage. They truly can't see or comprehend that they *are* in bondage. When a blinding spirit has penetrated a person, we can't rationalize with them because a demonic spirit binds them. Oppressed and bound, they don't know they are being held captive.

Years ago, my husband told me that I had a spirit of control. I argued for years that I didn't have control. After all, I was casting control out of others; surely I would know if I had it myself. I knew instances when I was controlling in the past, and I knew where I had to watch out for pockets of control, yet I had no idea that control was still a large part of my life. I would deny it because I didn't see it—a blinding spirit oppressed me. Just as horses wear blinders to restrict their vision so they can't see their surroundings, the enemy attacked me with a blinding spirit to restrict and obstruct my vision so I couldn't see it in myself. The Bible tells us:

> *And why do you see the speck that is in your brother's eye, but do not consider the plank that is in your own eye? Or how will you say to your brother, "Let me pull the speck out of your eye," when a log is in your own eye? You hypocrite! First take the plank out of your own eye, and then you will see clearly to take the speck out of your brother's eye.* (Matthew 7:3–5)

I was taking out other people's strongholds when I didn't see my own. It is common for people to want to learn about strongholds because they think everyone else has this problem, but they aren't looking at what may be manifesting through themselves. Demonic spirits are attempting to blind us from the truth. I can understand how people can be so deceived because as it is activating, you really don't realize it.

> PEOPLE OFTEN WANT TO LEARN ABOUT STRONGHOLDS BECAUSE THEY THINK EVERYONE ELSE HAS THIS PROBLEM, BUT THEY DON'T REALIZE IT'S MANIFESTING IN THEM.

PERSONAL

When we speak of personal issues, we want to be in control of our lives and our circumstances. We know we cannot control everything, but we just want some sense of control.

Before we continue, I want you to do this prophetic exercise that I myself did years ago and found very helpful.

FREEDOM APPLICATION

Be honest. In the first column, jot down where you trust God, or where you have trusted Him in the past, and He has proven to be faithful. In the second column, write where you don't trust God. Note anything and everything in both columns.

WHERE I TRUST GOD	WHERE I DON'T TRUST GOD

I want you to look at your column for "Where I Trust God." Place it as a keepsake in your mind for every time you trusted God. Remembering His faithfulness will help you to move out of mind lockdown when you don't know how it will happen.

Now look at the places where you don't trust God. Use those areas to co-labor with the Holy Spirit to move through your deliverance. Eventually, you will transfer them to the column for "Where I Trust God."

Mark this page and use it as a journal over the years so that as you begin to trust God in these areas, you can come back and see the progress you have made.

THE UNSEEN IS POWERFUL

The unseen spiritual realm is powerful, activating both angels and demons. We know that God, even though unseen, is on our side. We have another powerful, unseen spiritual force: our faith. Here are two translations of two verses from the Word of God:

+ *Now faith is the substance of things hoped for, the evidence of things not seen.* (Hebrews 11:1)

+ *Trusting is being confident of what we hope for, convinced about things we do not see.* (Hebrews 11:1 CJB)
+ *For we walk by faith, not by sight.* (2 Corinthians 5:7)
+ *For we live by trust, not by what we see.* (2 Corinthians 5:7 CJB)

Trust is about building an intimate relationship with the Lord so we can hear His voice at all times. We need to learn to listen to His voice during the chaos and the quiet times. Trust overflows from a personal relationship with Him and spending continual time in the secret place. If we aren't hearing from the Lord, it is probably because we are lacking in our God time.

> TRUSTING GOD IS BEING IN A PERPETUAL RELATIONSHIP
> WITH HIM, COMMUNING WITH HIM DAILY
> SO WE CAN INCREASE OUR DEPENDENCE ON HIM.

In my own life, I noticed that when God was silent, it was because I moved, but He never did. Trusting God is being in a perpetual relationship with Him, communing with Him daily so we can increase our dependence on Him. It is no different than with people. We have to spend more time with them and get to know them better in order to trust them. We cannot establish a great trust relationship with the Lord unless we have cultivated a personal relationship with Him.

RESULTS OF THE SECRET PLACE

I had to trust God when He told me to minister on a cruise ship when my husband and I had no desire to take such a voyage. I had to trust Him even though my extended family wasn't happy I would be away on the weekend we were celebrating Christmas. I remember sitting on the couch, staring up at the "Trust God" sign over my picture window and thinking about the conflict with my rescheduling our Christmas plans. I had purchased that sign to remind myself that I needed to learn to trust God.

Then the Lord spoke to me. "Kathy, will you trust Me?" He asked.

"I will trust You to the ends of this earth," I replied.

Making that statement was huge for me because I had previously gone through three intense trust journeys. My business card is shoved behind that sign as a prophetic act of trust. And so when the Lord told me to minister on a cruise, I took my team, my husband, and my daughter. Before we left, we knew there was a Category Four hurricane in the ocean, but we went anyway. We were aboard the cruise ship when it had to change course abruptly and go back to port. I was never in fear and kept trusting God. We grabbed a bite to eat as the hurricane sirens were going off inland.

After I was home for two weeks, I was sitting on the same couch, looking up at the "Trust God" sign, when I realized there was no fear in me. I thought about situations over the prior two weeks that normally would have created fear within me that had not affected me. Trusting God on a cruise ship during a hurricane had delivered me from fear. It was a prophetic act. Actions we take in the natural can break something loose in the spiritual. I could have never done it all without the abundant flow of hearing His voice in the secret place. Amid many storms with relationships and natural circumstances, I could hear His voice.

TWO AREAS WHERE WE DON'T TRUST GOD

There are two areas where it seems easier to believe in someone else's blessing but not our own: finances and healing. These are the biggest cases in which we don't trust God.

FINANCES

God is our provider. His name is *Jehovah Jireh*, the Lord Will Provide. In winning the battle over poverty and lack, we need to see God as the provider—not our spouses or our paychecks. If He cares for the birds of the air and provides for them, how much more will He care for us? (See Matthew 6:26.) Financial burdens are a worry on many people's minds and hearts. But man is not responsible for our protection and our provision. That is Father God's job, something He revealed to me years ago.

> MAN IS NOT RESPONSIBLE FOR OUR PROTECTION AND OUR PROVISION.
> THAT IS FATHER GOD'S JOB.

Fear of finances is usually the result of a lie that you believe. What is yours? Is it fear of not paying off your bills, being in debt, or not having enough money to pay for food, clothing, or shelter? Once you identify the lie, you need to go further and discover the root. Were you raised in poverty, have you struggled financially, or did you have money and lose it? Can you separate the truth of what God's Word says from the lie? Where are you not trusting the Lord to be your provider? Why do you not believe He will provide for all of your needs?

Let's break this down. If you have anxiety or worry about finances, there is a thought plaguing your mind that your situation isn't going to change or that money will not come forth. This thought is a lie, and behind the lie is fear. What do you fear? Behind the fear is a place you aren't trusting. Why aren't you trusting? What is the root? Did you grow up in poverty? Did someone embezzle money from your company? What happened in the past to make you doubt or fear not having enough money? You must be healed from the root cause, the beginning reason that instilled the fear for lack of financial provision. Once you find the entry point, you can begin to work through the questions embedded in this chapter to release freedom.

FREEDOM APPLICATION

We have a trust issue when we are in fear or mind bondage. Finding our trust issue will give us something to target to work out our freedom. When we struggle with a mind battle, we are believing a thought that's pulling us into negativity. Behind the negative thought is a lie we perceive as reality. The lie is being fueled by something we fear. Ultimately, we fear because we aren't trusting God for something in our life.

Let's discover the lie in our life so we can replace it with the truth.

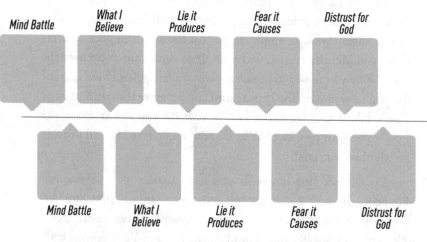

HEALING

Jesus came to be our healer. (See Isaiah 53:5.) The atonement didn't merely purchase our salvation to live eternally; it redeemed us from sickness and disease so healing could manifest in our lives. One of God's names is *Jehovah Rapha*, the Lord Who Heals.

A famous preacher once said, "If you can believe for your healing, then stand in faith for it. If you can't believe for it, go and see a medical doctor." He encouraged people to increase in their faith for healing, but seek medical help while waiting for their faith to increase.

As we enter the end times, the Holy Spirit has been speaking to me about rooting out all fear so we manifest faith. We need to start to do that now so that when times get hard, we can rely on the testimonies of what He did in the past to believe in our current situation.

Fear and anxiety often set in when it comes to health and medical ailments. You may have a strong faith in healing, but it tends to rub off if you don't stand firm when everyone else around you is in fear. Fear for health issues ultimately stems from not trusting Jesus to be your Healer and Father God to be your protector.

> FEAR FOR HEALTH ISSUES ULTIMATELY STEMS FROM NOT TRUSTING JESUS TO BE YOUR HEALER AND FATHER GOD TO BE YOUR PROTECTOR.

We often put more faith in medical doctors, prescriptions, and the media's so-called experts rather than trusting Jesus to heal and protect us. A chief part of His ministry while on this earth was to provide physical healing to those who came to Him for help. One of the reasons we don't trust in Him is because fear and anxiety lead us into stinking thinking. We are afraid of being sick, and our minds exaggerate our medical challenges and think about the worst-case scenarios.

Jesus is our healer. That is undebatable. He came to heal us—body, mind, and soul. Why can't we just accept it? We get in fear, stress, worry, and anxiety, which aggravates our emotions and physical symptoms. Our imagination goes wild, and we begin to feel false manifestations due to our fears. If a friend comes into your house and says, "I have mites," what do you do? You instantly start feeling itchy from stress, anxiety, and fear. The mind battles we suffer will increase if we don't seek inner healing.

If you are feeling fear because of an emotional or physical health issue, there are two primary keys to use to manifest your freedom:

1. Testify about instances where Jesus healed you in the past. Confess your past victory out of your mouth so you can hear your faith and remember that testimony as symptoms manifest and your mind is tormented.

2. Capture every thought. Get up, worship, and cast down every vain imagination.

As with the other emotional bondages discussed in this chapter, lack of healing also has a root cause we need to identify to receive our freedom.

FREEDOM APPLICATION

Let's go through the backward steps to freedom. Use the following chart to diagram your answers. What do you fear regarding a medical diagnosis, or where do you doubt you will be healed? What lie do you believe? What Scripture can you attach to believe Jesus is your healer? Why can't you trust that Scripture or trust Jesus to be a healer? Do you have a trauma in your past regarding medical treatment or health ailments from which you need healing—a physical infirmity, mind affliction, or torment?

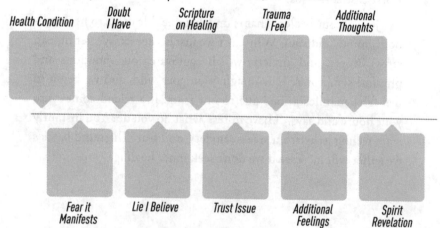

Health Condition	Doubt I Have	Scripture on Healing	Trauma I Feel	Additional Thoughts

Fear it Manifests	Lie I Believe	Trust Issue	Additional Feelings	Spirit Revelation

If you have a lot of medical or health trauma, compile a list and ask the Holy Spirit about each specific event, condition, treatment, or diagnosis and if you need healing prayer to root out the torment, sickness, or disease. Pray right now and command, "Every spirit of infirmity, leave me in Jesus's name." Declare, "By Christ's stripes, I am healed." (See Isaiah 53:5.)

I know the torment of having the enemy lock your mind, emotionally and spiritually paralyzing you regarding health ailments and physical infirmities. You think the worst and can't get your mind in the right direction. Friends, you've got to fight when you don't feel like fighting, and you've got to pray when you don't feel like praying. The only thing you can do is decree through the torment until the torment ends. I assure you that you *can* be free. I'm living proof of that. If He can set me free, He can set *you* free!

PROPHETIC ACTIVATION

IDENTIFY THE BATTLE

Every battle you initially face is rooted in a place where you lack trust. Trust is the hardest part because you must release and let go of all control, stress, worry, fear, and every other negative emotion within your soul. However, as you trust the Lord, additional blessings will be released. You will discover spiritual growth, a renewal of purpose, and every good and perfect gift He has for you. (See James 1:17.) Take a moment and journal all the ways you have not trusted Him, and everything you have trusted Him for that He has provided. Work on it as the Holy Spirit leads you and celebrate your victory where you do trust the Lord.

FORGIVE AND REPENT

It is not easy thinking we don't trust the Lord. The Bible says, *"The truth shall set you free"* (John 8:32). We know this is talking about the Word, but I also believe the truth sets us free when we see the root of our problem: a lack of trust in our heavenly Father.

Pray this prayer of forgiveness:

Heavenly Father, please forgive me for not trusting You. I know You have my best interests in mind. I repent of doubt and unbelief, and I ask for Your forgiveness. I want to trust You. Holy Spirit, root out any feelings I have that do not align with the Word of God. Help me to trust You. Thank You for Your love.

TARGET THE BATTLE AND BREAK AGREEMENT

I break agreement with comparing my heavenly Father to people. He is not like people, and I can trust Him completely. I command my soul and spirit to come into alignment with the Word of God. I speak and decree that I have abundant faith and trust. I speak and decree that I listen to the Lord and respond with obedience and discipline when He asks me to trust Him.

WARFARE PRAYER DECLARATIONS

- I proclaim that my trust for the Lord is increasing.
- I decree that when God asks me to take a step of faith, I respond with a joyful heart.
- I command doubt, unbelief, and distrust to leave me, in Jesus's name.
- I declare that I will not allow people to influence my decisions, and I will trust the Lord.
- I bind and restrict a spirit of fear and release trust and faith into my heart and soul.

RELEASE DELIVERANCE

Jesus was in the ministry of deliverance and cast out evil spirits. You are walking out your mind bondage now. One of the keys to getting free and staying free is to cast out the correlating spirit that could be manifesting. Pray audibly and command any of the following spirits to leave: lying, depression, worry, stress, anxiety, fear, mind-binding, torment, unforgiveness, and offense. Declare, "Spirit of _____, I cast you out, in Jesus's name."

REMOVE THE BATTLE

Take some time to remember all the places and ways you have trusted the Lord. Where has He truly come through for you? He is a sovereign God who loves you so much. Can you see that He takes care of you? How can you take what He has done in the past and believe He will do it presently and in the future so you can release trust in your life?

PROPHETIC APPLICATION

1. What has the Lord been asking you to do that you have avoided? Activate it.

2. Where do you have fear that prevents you from doing something beneficial? Take action and do something that would previously cause you to fear.

FREEDOM THOUGHT

Trust doesn't come naturally, but a spiritual breakthrough happens when you take a natural action!

10

OVERCOME SOULISH MENTALITIES

Our soul is the "me" part of us, the part that enables our flesh to act and react. I used to live in the flesh instead of walking in the Spirit. I liked to have my way and be in control. Fearful about finances and health ailments, I allowed my flesh to rule, which created mind torment.

Control and fear represent a lack of trust in our relationship with the Father. If we truly trusted God, we would walk in the Spirit and live as victors, not victims. The Bible says, "*I say then, walk in the Spirit, and you shall not fulfill the lust of the flesh*" (Galatians 5:16).

> IF WE ARE OVERLY CONSUMED BY FEELINGS, FINANCES, FEAR, OR OFFENSE, WE DON'T HAVE OUR ATTENTION AND AFFECTION ON OUR HEAVENLY FATHER.

The lust of the flesh is anything we focus on more than God. If we are overly consumed by feelings, finances, fear, or offense, we don't have our attention and affection on our heavenly Father. Colossians 3:2 says, "*Set your affection on things above, not on things on earth.*" Our thinking gets sidetracked when we focus on what we don't have instead of what we do. Our affections are focused on the comforts of this world, and we live for earth instead of the kingdom.

However, we are kingdom citizens, and we should live for heaven. We are entitled to nothing on this earth; we are here to worship the Lord, serve God and people, and love God and love people. That's it—end of story. We are servants of the Most High King, so our attitude and affections should be to love and serve without expecting anything in return.

How can we do this? *We need to be free from ourselves.* Our souls become free when we have no expectations of other people. Mind battles often occur because people disappoint us, hurt us, or don't live up to our expectations. We can't control other people. The sooner we accept that they are not our responsibility and release disappointment, the sooner we can manifest change in our own hearts, which will in turn release freedom in our minds.

We hold ourselves in bondage because we want to change other people. We get stressed out because they won't pursue the Lord as we do, offer us an apology, or do something we want. It is a battle that rages within...but it is a battle *we* created because of false responsibility for another person that we take upon ourselves. We aren't responsible for other people's behavior or actions. We are only responsible for our own. Before we can set others free, we need to understand our soul's operation so we can control what we do.

WE ARE THREE-PART BEINGS

Understanding how we are made and designed is crucial in overcoming mental blockages. The Bible identifies us as three-part beings:

May the very God of peace sanctify you completely. And I pray to God that your whole spirit, soul, and body be preserved blameless unto the coming of our Lord Jesus Christ.

(1 Thessalonians 5:23)

I often wish I wasn't flesh. I just want to be spirit so that my feelings don't get hurt and I never arise in the flesh. Unfortunately, that is not the case. But I've had visions of being in heaven, dancing and worshipping in spirit only. It is so freeing!

As humans, we have a body, a spirit, and a soul. These three parts are connected, but they are separate.

THREE-PART BEING

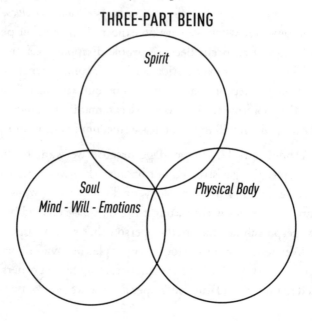

PHYSICAL BODY

We were made in the very image of God, and we have a physical body created by Him.

Then God said, "Let us make man in our image, after our likeness, and let them have dominion over the fish of the sea, and over the birds of the air, and over the livestock, and over all the earth, and over every creeping thing that creeps on the earth." So God created man in His own image; in the image of

God He created him; male and female He created them.
(Genesis 1:26–27)

We have a natural, physical body that includes our organs, eyes, skin, bones, and every other part of us. Our body facilitates life. It can be attacked with physical infirmities or by demonic entities. It is the earth suit we use to host our spirit man and our soul. And it is also a temple of the Holy Spirit.

> OUR BODY FACILITATES LIFE;
> IT IS THE EARTH SUIT WE USE TO HOST OUR SPIRIT MAN AND OUR
> SOUL. IT IS ALSO A TEMPLE OF THE HOLY SPIRIT.

Do you not know that your body is the temple of the Holy Spirit, who is in you, whom you have received from God, and that you are not your own? You were bought with a price. Therefore glorify God in your body and in your spirit, which are God's. (1 Corinthians 6:19–20)

Someday, our body will die and decay in a grave, but the good news is that our soul and our spirit, which comprise who we are, will live forever!

SPIRIT MAN

There is a spirit inside of us, and the Bible tells us this very clearly. *"But there is a spirit in man, and the breath of the Almighty gives him understanding"* (Job 32:8). Our heavenly Father loves us so much that He puts His Spirit in us and designed our spirits to connect with His Spirit. I love how *The Complete Jewish Bible* puts this, saying the Lord *"formed the spirit inside human beings"* (Zechariah 12:1 cjb). He not only created us in His image, as we are told in Genesis 1, but He also created our spirit man inside of us.

God is Spirit, and we are spirit. One of the chief ways that we can connect our spirit to His Spirit is through worship. *"God is Spirit, and those who worship Him must worship Him in spirit and truth"* (John 4:24). It brings forth great freedom when we worship Him in spirit and connect our spirit to His. It is one of the ways we feel God's presence.

I believe we are a conduit of the Holy Spirit through which the Spirit can be poured out into the world. Our bodies and hands are a platform and vessel for Him. If I touch you in prayer, you should feel Him through me. We should be so full of His Spirit that people can feel it, see it, and sense it. Romans 8:16 says, *"The Spirit Himself bears witness with our spirits that we are the children of God."*

People should feel God's presence within us, not all of the emotional and mental bondage. *"But he who is joined to the Lord becomes one spirit with Him"* (1 Corinthians 6:17). We should be one with the Lord and want the Lord to be one with us. We should be so completely intertwined in the Word, worship, and prayer that we dwell and exist with the Lord. We should be in constant communion with Him, in a perpetual study of His Word, and living out what we receive through revelation.

As Jesus walked this earth, He was like us with a physical body, soul, and spirit. I love the story in Mark 1 in which Jesus cleanses a leper.

> *A leper came to Him, pleading with Him and kneeling before Him, saying, "If You are willing, You can make me clean." Then Jesus, moved with compassion, extended His hand and touched him, and said to him, "I will. Be clean." As soon as He had spoken, the leprosy immediately departed from him, and he was cleansed.*   (Mark 1:40–42)

Jesus put His three-part being into this healing. He was moved with compassion, which is an emotion, part of the soul. He said He was willing, which was the Spirit. And Jesus stretched out His hand and touched the leper, which involved the Lord's physical body. This is an outstanding example of how we should be all-in like Jesus. We should act from every part of our three-part being—soul, spirit, and body.

When He died, Jesus further reaffirmed He was part spirit as He cried out on the cross.

> And Jesus cried out with a loud voice, "Father, into Your hands I commit My spirit." Having said this, He gave up the spirit.   (Luke 23:46)

The battle we encounter is in our minds and emotions. Whether there's a stronghold in our mind or an evil spirit has penetrated our body, the problem is in our soul, not our spirit. Demonic spirits cannot enter our spirit. There is a common misunderstanding that a Christian cannot have a demon because a demon can't occupy our spirits. Indeed, a demon cannot occupy our spirit man, but it can occupy our soul and our physical body to demonically oppress us.

> WHETHER THERE'S A STRONGHOLD IN OUR MIND OR
> AN EVIL SPIRIT HAS PENETRATED OUR BODY,
> THE PROBLEM IS IN OUR SOUL, NOT OUR SPIRIT.

Some also argue that a demon can't possess a Christian. And it's true that Christians cannot be fully taken over, but the word possessed means "influenced or controlled by something (such as an evil spirit, a passion, or an idea)."[8] We can fall under the influence of a demon or react with an emotional response of anger or fear. A demon can occupy or possess that part of you where you have fallen under its influence through an emotional ailment or physical infirmity.

---

8. www.merriam-webster.com/dictionary/possessed.

If you desire to overcome strongholds in your life, I want you to discern if that emotional stronghold could be a demonic spirit. Take a moment and think about areas where you haven't been able to receive complete freedom. What is the roadblock? Why aren't you receiving deliverance? If you've tried to get free to no avail, could the missing element be that you need to cast out a demonic spirit?

YOUR SOUL

Your soul is what I call the "me" part—your mind, will, and emotions. It is who you are and who God is creating you to be. Your soul is where you feel, think, and make decisions. It is also the part of you where demons and strongholds can infiltrate.

We can see through Scripture that the soul is where we need deliverance:

+ *Then called I upon the name of the* LORD: *"O* LORD, *I plead with You, deliver my soul."* (Psalm 116:4)

+ *For You have delivered my soul from death, my eyes from tears, and my feet from falling.* (Psalm 116:8)

+ *Bring my soul out of prison, that I may praise Your name.* (Psalm 142:7)

+ *Revive me, O* LORD, *for Your name's sake, for Your righteousness' sake bring my soul out of trouble.* (Psalm 143:11)

Can you relate to these Scriptures of being in prison and distress, desiring deliverance for your soul?

These psalms indicate deep soul wounds. There are wounds in our souls—our minds, wills, and emotions—that require healing and deliverance. In this book, we will heal soul wounds and cast out demonic spirits so we can walk in freedom and victory, being the overcomers that the Bible talks about. (See Revelation 12:11.) God created us to be victorious, not victimized. Part of our deliverance is shifting directions and choosing to think differently. We can't blame everything on everyone else; we must take responsibility for ourselves. We can control our thoughts when we choose to do so. It takes effort, but it can be accomplished as we learn together and practice.

When our soul is afflicted, it can feel like death, or as if we were in a pit. The dark place in our soul feels similar to Sheol. The Psalms again refer to how we can feel.

+ *For the enemy has persecuted my soul; he has crushed my life down to the ground; he has made me to dwell in darkness, as those who have been long dead.* (Psalm 143:3)

+ *For my soul is full of troubles, and my life draws near to Sheol.* (Psalm 88:3)

+ *Unless the* Lord *had been my help, my soul would have lived in the land of silent death.* (Psalm 94:17)

+ *But God shall redeem my soul from the power of Sheol, for He shall receive me.* (Psalm 49:15)

I want to reiterate a previous point that the enemy in Psalm 143:3 comes after our soul. It is our soul that is attacked, so we cannot have the excuse that we are spiritually dry. Our soul and spirit man are separate. When we go through emotional battles, it can feel like death, a deep, dark place. We need to go on the offensive in our souls. When I felt myself going into a dark place, I contacted a couple of friends for accountability and prayer. I survived that warfare attack and came out stronger.

RESTORATION OF THE SOUL

Our Father cares deeply about bringing restoration to our souls. As we cry out to Him, He will deliver us. I think we get so focused on our spirit man and connecting with the Father that we don't consider that He made our soul and wants us to be emotionally healthy. Read the book of Psalms. In this one, notice how He delivers us when we cry out to Him:

> I love the LORD, because He has heard my voice and my supplications. Because He has inclined His ear to me, therefore I will call upon Him as long as I live. The cords of death encircled me, and the pains of Sheol took hold of me; I found trouble and sorrow. Then called I upon the name of the LORD: "O LORD, I plead with You, deliver my soul." Gracious is the LORD, and righteous; indeed, our God is merciful. The LORD protects the simple; I was brought low, and He helped me. Return to your rest, O my soul; for the LORD has vindicated you. For You have delivered my soul from death, my eyes from tears, and my feet from falling. I will walk before the LORD in the land of the living. (Psalm 116:1–9)

Calling out to our God can be difficult when we feel defeated, victimized, or fearful. Our emotions get the best of us. We go to a place we shouldn't in our minds, focusing more on the negative than trying to press through to the goodness of our delivering Savior. We know we have to something to do about our situation, but what?

> IF WE PRESS THROUGH TO OUR BREAKTHROUGH AND REPEATEDLY GO BEFORE THE THRONE OF GOD, HE WILL GIVE US WHAT WE NEED.

So often, we seek a deliverance ministry or visit a counselor to talk out our problems. We want someone else to fix us. But it's *our* responsibility to break free and help ourselves by seeking God. We have the greatest team of three on our side: Father God, Jesus His Son, and the Holy Spirit. Jesus is the Deliverer, and the Holy Spirit is our Guide. If we press through to our breakthrough and repeatedly go before the throne of God, He will give us what we need. Deliverance is *"the children's bread"* (Matthew 15:26). We would get far if we had the faith of the Canaanite woman.

Then Jesus went from there and departed into the regions of Tyre and Sidon. There, a woman of Canaan came out of the same regions and cried out to Him, saying, "Have mercy on me, O Lord, Son of David. My daughter is severely possessed by a demon." But He did not answer her a word. And His disciples came and begged Him, saying, "Send her away, for she cries out after us." But He answered, "I was sent only to the lost sheep of the house of Israel." Then she came and worshipped Him, saying, "Lord, help me." But He answered, "It is not fair to take the children's bread and to throw it to dogs." She said, "Yes, Lord, yet even dogs eat the crumbs that fall from their masters' table." Then Jesus answered her, "O woman, great is your faith. Let it be done for you as you desire." And her daughter was healed instantly.   (Matthew 15:21–28)

The Canaanite woman pressed in with faith, and Jesus answered her prayer.

My friend, your deliverance is in your hands. Your freedom comes from learning. Your mind gets renewed by thinking positive and filling yourself up with the Word of God. It is at your disposal. What are you going to do to take it by force?

From the days of John the Baptist until now, the kingdom of heaven has forcefully advanced, and the strong take it by force.   (Matthew 11:12)

We have to take our minds back by force! We have to believe in ourselves and our deliverance, knowing we can change. The Lord can strengthen and deliver our souls. This isn't something waiting for us after we get to heaven and have our new, resurrected bodies; it is available right now, while we are breathing and living on this earth. We don't have to wait for wholeness. You can restore your mind when you seek the Holy Spirit.

On the day I called, You answered me, and strengthened me in my soul. (Psalm 138:3)

O LORD, You have brought up my soul from the grave; You have kept me alive, that I should not go down to the pit. (Psalm 30:3)

Our soul waits for the LORD; He is our help and our shield. (Psalm 33:20)

My soul, wait silently for God, for my hope is from Him. (Psalm 62:5)

My soul waits in silence on God alone; from Him comes my salvation. (Psalm 62:1)

He restores my soul; He leads me in paths of righteousness for His name's sake. (Psalm 23:3)

Not every battle has a spiritual origin and can be fought with spiritual tactics. There is a connection between what we do physically and emotionally, so we need to have tools to fight each battle. We all face our own battle and have warfare techniques that work best for us. No matter if we are bound with a demonic spirit or have had all evil spirits cast out, walking out our freedom includes changing thought patterns and behaviors. There are things we can do in the natural to lessen the mind battle we face.

Whether or not you believe in the ministry of deliverance, you can take these steps to overcome mind battles:

1. Talk yourself out of it. Rationalize the reality of the outcome. Talk yourself happy. Convince yourself it is your imagination or a lie you believe and move on.

2. Live! Don't allow your thoughts to control you; control your thoughts instead. Detrimental thoughts can

prevent you from doing something good. Enjoy life! Take a chance! Do what you fear! Don't allow your mind to stop you from doing what you want and being who you want to be.

3. Exercise. Get up and get moving. Take a walk or go for a jog and get your body moving to release feel-good endorphins and get your mind off what is worrying and distracting you.

4. Breathe! Go outside and breathe in fresh air. Clear your head, go sit by the water and relax, enjoy nature and the things you like. Five minutes of outside air can change your thoughts, release peace, and refocus your thinking.

5. Find an accountability partner, someone you can talk to whom you trust. Let them know you are worrying about something. They can hold you accountable to remove that thought and refocus your mind, speak sense into you, and give you a push in the right direction. They can also be your cheerleader and lift you up without coddling you.

6. Play music and worship. Hymns and spiritual or uplifting music can change your mood and draw you closer to God. If you are feeling down, play something that transitions you to peace.

7. Find a few sayings that encourage you and speak them aloud, such as:

   a. You can do this!

   b. Change your thinking, change your mind.

   c. Positivity over negativity.

   d. I'm dismissing negativity and gaining a new thought.

   e. My mind is renewed.

8. Be thankful and give praise. Instead of focusing on the negative, look at your situation and be appreciative of the good things you have.

9. Be love. Release love into other people's lives. Give love and receive love. Love changes everything, so focus on love as the core of who you are.

PROPHETIC ACTIVATION

IDENTIFY THE BATTLE

Your freedom is sometimes contingent on the information you receive. Now that you know God cares about your soul, and you can better identify the difference between your soul and your spirit, can you pinpoint the battle more accurately? The battle within your soul doesn't have to consume you. Once you identify the stronghold, you can establish a battle plan to remove it.

FORGIVE AND REPENT

Where do you need to forgive yourself for fleshly actions and thoughts? Where do you need to repent and change your thinking for believing you can't be set free? In the process of mind bondage, you can feel defeated and find it easier to believe in another person's freedom rather than your own. Forgive yourself for feeling victimized.

Pray audibly this prayer of forgiveness:

Dear Jesus, forgive me for times I didn't believe I could be healed and didn't pursuing my healing. I believe my dreams can still come true. I want to renew my mind. Please convict me, Holy Spirit, when I feel defeated. I am not a victim but victorious. Help me to forgive myself for staying in guilt, condemnation, shame, blame, and regret, in Jesus's name. Amen.

TARGET THE BATTLE AND BREAK AGREEMENT

Speak out and decree:

I proclaim, release, and break agreement with every attack against my mind, will, and emotions, and command all attacks to stop. I declare I will change, repent, turn around, and arise above my mind battles. I pronounce and decree that I am not defeated, and I can and will change. Victory is imminent for me! I will have prosperity in my mind and thinking. I am established in every good thing that the Lord has for me.

RELEASE DELIVERANCE

Jesus was in the ministry of deliverance and cast out evil spirits. You are walking out your mind bondage now. One of the keys to getting free and staying free is to cast out the correlating spirit that could be manifesting. Pray audibly and command any of the following spirits to leave: lying, depression, worry, stress, anxiety, fear, mind-binding, torment, unforgiveness, and offense. Declare, "Spirit of _____, I cast you out, in Jesus's name."

WARFARE PRAYER DECLARATIONS

+ I command my soul to align with my spirit man and my spirit man to align with the Holy Spirit.

+ I order my mind, will, and emotions to align with the Word of God and the will of God for my life.

+ I instruct my mind to react with positive thoughts. I will transition my thinking toward good and God.

+ I bind and restrict fleshly actions and reactions. I choose to walk in the Spirit.

+ I bind and restrict my flesh from activating and decree that I am led by the Holy Spirit.

REMOVE THE BATTLE

It can be difficult to believe we can be different when we have been one way for years. We can also face an identity issue, not knowing who we will be without the bondage. When a friend of mine drove cancer patients to treatment facilities, most of them didn't want her to pray for healing for their bodies. They said they received attention due to their condition, and it gave them something to talk about. Do you have a similar battle in your mind that needs to be removed? Do you truly want to be different?

PROPHETIC APPLICATION

1. How can you establish your mind to think different? Are there additional books and resources you can use to assist you in your journey?

2. How can you change your thinking to positive thoughts?

FREEDOM THOUGHT

Every moment we waste focusing on how our soul needs to be satisfied is a moment we lose for operating in the Spirit and releasing the love and goodness of God to others.

11

CUT OFF THE ROOT

I was bound in fears for years. As a child, I observed fear, and I was taught to fear. When you see it modeled, hear it spoken out, and internalize reactions to situations based on fear, it becomes you. Fear seemed like a normal response in our home, and I didn't know how to behave any differently. While I wouldn't say fear ruled in every area of my life, my family gravitated toward it. I didn't feel debilitated by fear, but I remember being fearful throughout my life.

Generational curses attack us physically and emotionally. We must cut off the root to change our mentality. I was trained to be fearful and have a negative mindset, but our brains are ever changing, and we can reprogram them if we make the effort. One of the ways I did this was by quoting this Scripture to myself:

For you did not receive a spirit of slavery to bring you back again into fear; on the contrary, you received the Spirit, who makes us sons and by whose power we cry out, "Abba!" (that is, "Dear Father!"). (Romans 8:15 cjb)

This transformative verse saved my life! I would repeatedly tell myself that my heavenly Father had adopted me, that I was not a product of my past or my childhood. I constantly renewed my mind and cast down every thought.

Generational curses come from our family line. The fact that our parents never sought their inner healing and attempted to remove the curse contributes to our problems. We cannot blame them, however, since we live in a fallen world where the demonic realm is active, and people haven't been taught to seek their healing and break the curse.

> WE CANNOT BLAME OUR PARENTS FOR GENERATIONAL CURSES SINCE WE LIVE IN A FALLEN WORLD WHERE THE DEMONIC REALM IS ACTIVE.

Mind renewal begins with you seeing and perceiving your situation differently. Transform your mind by realizing that you are not under a curse but redeemed. *"Christ has redeemed us from the curse of the law by being made a curse for us"* (Galatians 3:13). New strategies and thought processes will help you move forward and not get stuck in the past. You are redeemed from generational curses by the blood of Jesus. Transforming your mind to the Word and not seeking to blame the world will release freedom.

Ultimately, we live in a world under demonic influence. Separate the principality from the person. Dislike the principality of fear or the generational curse, but don't blame your parents; blame the enemy and the fallen world we live in. Direct your pain to the spiritual realm and target it forcefully in prayer to destroy every bondage in your life that was passed down through your bloodline.

To guard and protect myself as I walked out my freedom, I had to choose what conversations to have with family members. When something from their mouths to my ears triggered fear, I had to rebuke it and dismiss it. It was difficult to get free because family conversations would routinely result in fear triggers. I longed for freedom from worries about health ailments, storms, and finances, but even when I reached adulthood, family discussions pulled that trigger again. I had to consistently remind myself that I was a daughter of the King, that I had a royal bloodline. I had to limit conversations and put up some self-protective walls.

Generational fear followed me on health concerns, death, heights, storms, vehicle accidents, and poverty. I saw fear exhibited in our family, and it became me. It owned me for a while, but it no longer possesses me. It may attempt to oppress me—the strongman usually will try to attack again—but I now know the tools and strategies for my freedom.

YOUR FIRST LINE OF DEFENSE

As we attempt to gain freedom, we need to protect our minds and our hearts. The powerful Word of God is our first line of defense and can be used to renew our minds. Romans 8:15 was crucial to me; I found it helpful to say out loud, "I am adopted into the family of Father God. I have a new bloodline." I would look at my veins and say, "The blood of Jesus flows through my veins." We have been grafted onto Jesus based on Romans 11:17. I would picture a vine with many interconnected branches and look at my veins as a visual reminder of my union with Him. It was my way of *"bringing every thought into captivity to the obedience of Christ"* (2 Corinthians 10:5).

> A MIND BATTLE CAN BE A LEARNED TRAIT, A SOUL TIE,
> THE RESULT OF A TRAUMA, A GENERATIONAL CURSE, AN EMOTIONAL
> AILMENT, OR HAVE SOME OTHER SOURCE.

Generational curses can be broken, but first, we must determine if a curse is indeed at work. When dealing with mind battles, they can be a learned trait, a soul tie, the result of a trauma, a generational curse, an emotional ailment, or have another cause in the natural. Every mind battle is unique and has a singular origin. Since we were created in the image of God, we weren't meant to have mind battles. Therefore, we need to find the root and cut it off to walk out in freedom effectively.

The Word of God says that He will visit the parents' iniquities upon the children, grandchildren, and great-grandchildren. (See Exodus 20:5; 34:7.) But we are redeemed from the curse; it was taken at the cross.

> *Christ has redeemed us from the curse of the law by being made a curse for us—as it is written, "Cursed is everyone who hangs on a tree."* (Galatians 3:13)

The Bible tells us to walk out our salvation.

> *Therefore, my beloved, as you have always obeyed, not only in my presence, but so much more in my absence, work out your own salvation with fear and trembling.* (Philippians 2:12)

The word "salvation" in Greek (*Strong's* G4991) means deliverance. Therefore, we need to work and walk out our deliverance. Even though Jesus took the curse, we have to remove it. We do this through the power of our words, by breaking agreement with the curse when we identify it.

Generational curses can manifest with depression, fear, stress, anxiety, and worry. However, the curses don't have to overtake us. If we have been raised with emotional ailments and know the generational curses that afflict us, we don't have to suffer with them like our parents did. Just because a doctor has diagnosed you with an emotional condition doesn't mean that you can't be healed, change your brain, and break the curse.

CURSES DEFINED

Curses aim to destroy, defile, or desecrate the sacred and holy. We are supposed to be sacred and holy, set apart for God. The dictionary defines *sacred* as "dedicated or set apart for the service or worship of a deity." We are set apart *for* God. It was not His intention for us to be set apart *from* Him by experiencing mind bondages.

We have been cursed in our bloodlines, and now it's time to make sure we have been redeemed from the curse, as the Bible says, "*Christ has redeemed us from the curse of the law by being made a curse for us*" (Galatians 3:13). There is freedom and deliverance available through Christ. Breaking generational curses isn't as easy as speaking once out loud, "I command all generational curses to be gone in Jesus's name." The Word of God says He will bring the iniquity upon the generations.

> *You shall not bow down to them or serve them; for I, the LORD your God, am a jealous God, visiting the iniquity of the fathers on the children to the third and fourth generation of them who hate Me, and showing lovingkindness to thousands of them who love Me and keep My commandments.*
> (Exodus 20:5–6)

> *The LORD passed by before him, and proclaimed, "The LORD, the LORD God, merciful and gracious, slow to anger, and abounding in goodness and truth, keeping mercy for thousands, forgiving iniquity and transgression and sin, but who will by no means clear the guilty, visiting the iniquity of fathers on the children and on the children's children, to the third and the fourth generation."*
> (Exodus 34:6–7)

I could not say just once, "Fear be gone," and have it instantly disappear out of my life. I had to work and walk through the process of freedom. God's Word tells us He visits the iniquity of the fathers upon the children. I had to break agreement, repent for my parents, and change the learned thinking patterns.

We have been redeemed from the curse and do not have to live with it. But that doesn't mean our generational curses all left when Jesus died on the cross. We may still suffer from our parents' emotional behaviors. If they all went away at the cross, we would already be living in total victory and freedom. As we diagram them and work through each one, we can be healed, delivered, and set free.

EXAMINING YOUR FAMILY TREE

We diagram our family tree to discover our lineage. We write down our relatives' names and how they were related to us. If we dig deeper, we usually discover where they came from. Our family trees can contain valuable information about our spiritual walk when we are seeking deliverance.

Have you ever thought about diagramming your family tree to help you discover the root of your emotional issues? Sometimes it can help you to look back in order to move forward.

> WHEN OUR PARENT HAS MANIFESTED FEAR, ANGER, OR CONTROL, WE OFTEN EXHIBIT THAT SAME BEHAVIOR THROUGH A GENERATIONAL CURSE AND OUR OBSERVATIONS OF THEM.

We can inherit emotional issues—such as depression, bipolar disorder, control, anger, and fear—in our generational lines. When our parent has manifested fear, anger, or control, we often exhibit that same behavior through a generational curse and our observations of their reactions and actions. We were a product of that curse, and we have learned the behaviors they have modeled for us. Over time, when we don't rebuke and renounce these negative issues, they become a stronghold, and we experience the manifestation of that generational curse.

How can we take what we know about our family line to bring forth deliverance from emotional strongholds? When I lead people through generational curses, it isn't as easy as saying, "All generational curses be gone in Jesus's name." We need to evaluate our ancestry, see if we can find the curse's entry point, or figure out if we ourselves are starting a new curse upon our descendants. I take people through diagramming a spiritual and physical family tree. This is just like a standard family tree, but we include any emotional ailment under each person's name.

FREEDOM APPLICATION

Here are some emotional ailments to look for to reveal generational curses:

Depression	Anger	Fear	Stress
Anxiety	Worry	Unworthy	Insecurity
Rejection	Hurt	Selfish	Critical
Judgmental	Irritability	Bitterness	Condemnation
Dishonesty	Hardheartedness	Stubborn	Guilt
Haughtiness	Helplessness	Hopelessness	Impatient
Intimidation	Jealousy	Legalism	Manipulation
Lying	Torment	Unfairness	Unforgiveness
Offense	Rejection	Control	Passive

Family Tree

Fill in your family tree to see what you may have inherited or what's been passed down from previous generations. Write down as many things as you can under each person's name. What commonalities are there? Now you have found the generational curses in your family line.

Pray and ask the Holy Spirit to guide you in prayer so that you can receive deliverance. What emotional ailment in your family tree affects you the most? If you can't hear from the Holy Spirit, you could choose to start with the easiest, so you see some immediate progress, or you could begin with the item that consumes your thoughts the most to obtain the greatest freedom.

FREEDOM APPLICATION

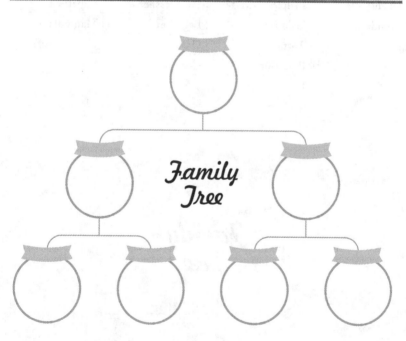

This inverted family tree starts with you. It enables you to see what you are passing down to your children and their children. We want to break agreement with any generational curses that have been or are being created.

I want to stress the importance of speaking these statements aloud so they release into the spiritual atmosphere. We need to renounce the curse, repent, and set things straight in the spirit realm by taking authority over where the curse began.

1. Repent for your generations. Say, "I repent for the sins of my grandparents, parents, and those before me. Father God, I ask for Your forgiveness on their behalf, and I rebuke and take authority over mind ailments that have triggered my family and me."

2. Repent for your actions. Speak, "Father, please forgive me for the behavior patterns, thoughts, and negative words I released. Forgive me for what I didn't know as well as what I knew and didn't try to stop and change."

3. Break agreement. Proclaim, "I break agreement with the generational curses. I call off any negative effect they have had on me. I command I will not participate in wrong actions and thoughts. I decree and declare I have broken every emotional curse against me."

I encourage you to also buy a copy of this book for your family members to use to break curses off their lives.

PROPHETIC ACTIVATION

IDENTIFY THE BATTLE

You inherit your parents' ears, eyes, hair, and other physical traits. Additionally, you can also inherit their emotional characteristics. What mannerisms, attitudes, and emotions do you have in common with your parents? Take note of where there may be a learned behavior pattern or thought life that you need to evict.

FORGIVE AND REPENT

You don't want to allow a seed of bitterness or offense to take root because of the discoveries you have made with these assignments. It is not about blaming your parents for any adverse behavior or thought pattern you have learned from them. Instead, the goal is to help you identify and remove these issues. Are there any feelings that you need to release due to the information you've uncovered in this chapter? Let's pray and make sure you have a clean heart moving forward.

Pray audibly this prayer of forgiveness:

Heavenly Father, I choose this day to forgive my parents and grandparents. I release them from any responsibility I feel they had in my bondage. I understand it was not their fault and resulted from a curse on our family line. I repent on their behalf and ask You to set my family and me free, in Jesus's name.

TARGET THE BATTLE

Speak out and decree:

I break agreement with every generational curse that I have inherited from my parents. Anything that was modeled and I took on as an unhealthy behavior pattern or attitude, I break and sever in Jesus's name. I speak and decree that I am redeemed from all curses and that my parents' sins don't have to follow me. I am a curse breaker and blessing maker from this day forward.

RELEASE DELIVERANCE

Jesus was in the ministry of deliverance and cast out evil spirits. You are walking out your mind bondage now. One of the keys to getting free and staying free is to cast out the correlating spirit that could be manifesting. Pray audibly and command any of the following spirits to leave: lying, depression, worry, stress, anxiety, fear, mind-binding, and torment. "Spirit of _____, I cast you out, in Jesus's name. I break and sever all generational curses. I decree and declare that I am set free from curses by the blood of the Lamb. I am no longer under the curse, but I am blessed, renewed, changed, and set free. I proclaim I will be a curse breaker and blessing maker in Jesus's name!"

WARFARE PRAYER DECLARATIONS

+ I expel every generational curse from my family line manifesting through me.

+ I eradicate every mind-binding spirit activating from my family line to me, and I completely destroy its effects on me.

+ I constrict every curse against me and command it to cease its activation.

+ I cast out every spirit of fear and every tormenting thought and spirit, in Jesus's name.

+ I announce that I am redeemed from the curse and that every curse is broken, in Jesus's name.

REMOVE THE BATTLE

You have been taught to remove the battle of the mind in your generational line. However, this exercise can additionally be used for physical ailments. Sickness and disease often have emotional roots. As you are healed from stress, anxiety, worry, or fear, your physical body can come into alignment. We know these things cause hypertension and diabetes. Try working on changing your emotional feelings and then chart another tree with physical infirmities. Work through them to receive your physical healing.

PROPHETIC APPLICATION

1. Determine that you will be a curse breaker and a blessing maker. What words and actions can you change to break off current bad habits in your family that are being modeled to your children?

2. How does your mind need to be renewed to know that you are a child of God and not a product of who your parents created you to be? How can you make sure you raise your children in such a way that they have individual personalities and identification in Christ?

FREEDOM THOUGHT

You are not a result of who your parents made you to be. You have been adopted by your heavenly Father and have His bloodline.

12

CHANGE YOUR WORDS, CHANGE YOUR MIND

Throughout the Gospels, we see the spiritual realm activated whenever Jesus spoke out. His words bound and restricted demons and brought healing to many people.

Years ago, I had to change my words because I was speaking out my fears. As I studied the ministry of deliverance, spiritual warfare, authority, and prayer, I learned how valuable my words were. I would not tell others how I was feeling physically or emotionally. Instead, I kept this information to myself so the enemy would not activate on my words negatively. The spirit realm is real, and angels and demons are waiting to act on our words. Once I became a spirit-filled Christian, I quickly learned the power of my tongue. (See Proverbs 18:21.) Changing my words changed my life and changed my mind.

Before we discuss how our own words affect our situation, let's explore the effects of other people's words on our lives. The very words that others speak can be the entry point to our battle.

HOW OTHERS' WORDS AFFECT US

The battle of our minds may be launched by words that others have said to us or about us. They fire off negative, hurtful statements that make us feel bad, with phrases such as these:

+ You're no good. You are never going to amount to anything.

+ You are overweight. All you do is eat.

+ You are selfish. You never change.

+ You always mess up and make mistakes. You can't do anything right.

Good or bad, words impact us for life. This is where the battle begins.

> **THE BATTLE OF OUR MINDS MAY BEGIN WITH NEGATIVE, HURTFUL STATEMENTS THAT OTHERS SAY ABOUT US.**

One battle I had to overcome in my mind was that I could never go out of the house, to the store, or even to the mailbox without makeup. Yes, something that simple built a stronghold in my mind. My dad is a wonderful person who makes me feel deeply loved. I never heard any nasty phrases like those I just mentioned from either parent. However, my dad would say, "Don't go out of the house without makeup. When you get married, you get up in the morning, put makeup on, and do your hair. Don't ever look like a slouchy housewife." (If only he saw me now, wearing leggings and no makeup!)

He didn't know saying that would establish a stronghold in my mind. My husband still talks about how I couldn't go out to the mailbox for years without makeup. I definitely wouldn't go to the store or allow friends or volunteers to see me without makeup. I had to break the stronghold in my mind. It didn't make me feel ugly or inferior, but I felt less confident and slightly self-conscious. Dad's words never hurt me, but they affected me and how I responded to them throughout life.

When we take in negative words that have been spoken to us, they latch on to us and become a stronghold. It can take us years to get these words out of our minds. They have become a truth in our lives, even though it's a distorted truth. Words hurt, and unfortunately, a part of us believes those words and lives them out.

I like the analogy my husband has used about the power of words to hurt us. He said one hurtful word, one mean sentence, or one offense is like a shot pellet fired from a BB gun. It hits you, and it stings. We can take a few hits and stings. It doesn't change our lives. But over time, those shot pellets can be gathered up and used to fill a shotgun shell. When that is fired, it's deadly. A few shot pellets fired from a BB gun will hurt, but a bunch of them fired from a shotgun will do a lot of damage. It can kill our emotions and feelings, our hope and our joy.

This is one of the ways we get in bondage over the years. Word curses and unpleasant statements build up in our minds and hearts, distorting the perception of who we are. We enter into a battle that we didn't bargain for and become captivated by the harmful thoughts.

The first step in overcoming this battle is to forgive the people who have hurt you by speaking word curses over your life or causing other offenses. Those people have been filling up a shotgun shell against you. Release them to the Lord.

YOUR WORDS PRODUCE LIFE

Of course, if other people's words can have power over us, imagine what our own words can do! We need to control our own words to keep our minds focused on good and God. Proverbs 18:21 says, *"Death and life are in the power of the tongue."* Our words come back to us and take flight in the spiritual realm. Our words have power and authority to bring forth good things. (See Luke 10:19; Genesis 1:26.) I know our words can also be used negatively because I have witnessed it.

In my book *Speak Out*,[9] I teach how Jesus used the power of His words to heal the sick and cast out demons. (See, for example, Matthew 8:16, 12:22; Mark 1:34, 3:10; Luke 4:39, 11:14, 13:12.) Father God used the power of words to create the earth and speak the universe into existence. (See Genesis 1.) If the power of our words can heal the sick and cast out demons (see Luke 10:19), how much more can our words produce in a positive or negative direction? When we speak of God's goodness, it increases our faith. When we speak out negatively, it can decrease our faith, causing confusion and mind bondage.

> SPEAKING OF GOD'S GOODNESS INCREASES OUR FAITH, WHILE SPEAKING NEGATIVELY CAN CAUSE CONFUSION AND MIND BONDAGE.

Did you ever stop to consider that the words you are speaking out may be making your situation worse?

I used to run Be Love Outreach and minister to those in need because of a physical impairment, emotional disability, or poverty. I remember one generous lady who said she had a physical disability. I never met her because she always left her donations on the porch for me to pick up. When she called or texted, she would say, "I'm the lady with a physical disability," which saddened me because she was more than able. She was one of the most giving persons in the community. She took her disability and used it as an ability to help others.

Are you identifying yourself as this woman did? Are the words you speak out and the way in which you perceive yourself holding you back from freedom?

Romans 8 is about the power of our thoughts, our old and new selves, and our minds, identification, and life. When I read this

---

9. Kathy DeGraw, *Speak Out: Releasing the Power of Declaring Prayer* (Lake Mary, FL: Creation House, 2017).

Scripture years ago, my spiritual eyes were opened to the truth of these passages. It is truth that we should impart into our souls.

> *For those who identify with their old nature set their minds on the things of the old nature, but those who identify with the Spirit set their minds on the things of the Spirit. Having one's mind controlled by the old nature is death, but having one's mind controlled by the Spirit is life and shalom. For the mind controlled by the old nature is hostile to God, because it does not submit itself to God's Torah — indeed, it cannot. Thus, those who identify with their old nature cannot please God. But you, you do not identify with your old nature but with the Spirit — provided the Spirit of God is living inside you, for anyone who doesn't have the Spirit of the Messiah doesn't belong to him. However, if the Messiah is in you, then, on the one hand, the body is dead because of sin; but, on the other hand, the Spirit is giving life because God considers you righteous. And if the Spirit of the One who raised Yeshua from the dead is living in you, then the One who raised the Messiah Yeshua from the dead will also give life to your mortal bodies through his Spirit living in you. So then, brothers, we don't owe a thing to our old nature that would require us to live according to our old nature. For if you live according to your old nature, you will certainly die; but if, by the Spirit, you keep putting to death the practices of the body, you will live.*
>
> (Romans 8:5–13 CJB)

Now that we are Christians, we don't identify with our old nature. We *"have become new"* (2 Corinthians 5:17). We are not meant to live focused on our old selves, sin, and what happened before we belonged to Jesus. When we repent, we turn around and change. We usually don't identify ourselves as a bank robber, a liar, or a car thief, so why would we title and identify ourselves as divorced, widowed, mentally ill, or depressed?

Those may be circumstances that happened to you or characteristics that have manifested through you, but it's not who you are. They no longer identify you because you are made new in Christ. Don't keep owning those circumstances by declaring them out of your mouth. Clean up your words, clean up your life! You are made in the image of God, and your identity is in Him, not what has happened to you or how you feel.

You are not depressed, mentally ill, or fearful; these are strongholds that are attacking you. It is not you. It is not who God created you to be. If you want to win the battle in your mind, you need to see yourself differently. You must refrain from speaking out negatively about yourself.

THE POWER OF YOUR WORDS

If other people's words can hurt us, our own words can certainly do the same. The words we choose can bring death or life to us.

> *I call heaven and earth to witnesses against you this day,*
> *that I have set before you life and death, blessing and curse.*
> *Therefore choose life, that both you and your descendants may*
> *live.*   (Deuteronomy 30:19)

Think about this. Many people have had negative words spoken to them by their parents. Those words were death and brought emotional curses, but we have the ability to break free. We can turn this situation around. More importantly, we can make sure we are passing only blessings, not curses, on to our own children.

My upbringing was responsible for my fear. If I had had some words bound and restricted, if I had not seen and heard so many actions of fear, I believe I would not have lived in fear for so long.

> YOU CAN BE A CURSE BREAKER AND A BLESSING MAKER.
> YOU CAN CREATE A DIVINE TURNAROUND IN YOUR FAMILY.

You have a chance to be a curse breaker and a blessing maker. You have an opportunity in this moment to make sure your children don't suffer. You are in a position to create a divine turnaround and shift in your family. Even if you have already spoken negative words or curses, you can retract them and change. It is never too late to change.

I also had to change midstream. I had to learn to say things differently and make sure I was releasing blessing and not fear. As I was writing this, I heard the Holy Spirit say, "Choose this day whom you will serve."

Now fear the Lord, *and serve Him with sincerity and faithfulness. Put away the gods your fathers served beyond the River and in Egypt. Serve the* Lord. *If it is displeasing to you to serve the* Lord, *then choose today whom you will serve, if it should be the gods your fathers served beyond the River or the gods of the Amorites' land where you are now living. Yet as for me and my house, we will serve the* Lord.

(Joshua 24:14–15)

Who will you serve? Are you going to serve the Lord wholeheartedly? If so, then give Him your mind. Don't spend another day renting out space to negative thoughts. Choose not to allow fear and depression to manifest, get up, and serve the Lord. You *"have the mind of Christ"* (1 Corinthians 2:16). Get busy for the kingdom and remove every obstacle that is holding you back from the fullness of God. There is so much potential in you. You can do this. I believe in you. Believe in yourself! Capture every thought! Change your words! Change your life!

WORDS CAN WIN OR LOSE THE BATTLE

I believe we increase our faith by hearing the Word of God. *"So then faith comes by hearing, and hearing by the word of God"* (Romans 10:17). I also believe we can use this Scripture to apply the words we speak out into the atmosphere. If we can speak out Scripture and have it bring forth life, can't we also speak out words that are detrimental to our hearing?

I used to speak death over my life without even realizing it. In a conversation with someone, I would jokingly say, "You're going to kill me for this," or "I'll kill you for that." Even though I didn't mean it, it was still a word curse that went into the spiritual atmosphere. One day while I was attending a conference, the speaker talked about spirits of death and then prayed for word curses and spirits of death to leave. I literally felt three spirits of death leave my body that day. Merely speaking in the natural had activated a word curse in the spiritual.

Throughout Scripture, we can see that there is power in the tongue and the words we speak, yet we often don't realize that the very words we speak can cycle back and put us in emotional turmoil and bondage. If we want to change our minds, we must be slow to speak. We will receive what we believe and what we speak. We cannot speak out that we are mentally ill, fearful, or depressed. The statements coming from our mouths must be powerful proclamations of the promises of God and encouraging words that truly represent the very best in us. We can change by speaking out the outcome of our positive expectations, not what we are experiencing. Remember, our brain is neuroplastic and ever-changing.

Jesus fought the devil with His words because He knew the power they held. When we look at the story of David and Goliath, it was a battle of words from the very beginning. Though huge in stature, Goliath was not engaging in a physical fight; instead, he was speaking threats, curses, and intimidation. He was using the power of his words. None of the Israelites wanted to fight Goliath. But David took him on, with his faith and the power of his words. He prophesied his victory in advance, proclaiming:

> The LORD who delivered me out of the paw of the lion and out of the paw of the bear, He will deliver me out of the hand of this Philistine. (1 Samuel 17:37)

Then armed with just a slingshot and five stones, David told Goliath:

> You come to me with a sword, a spear, and a shield, but I come to you in the name of the LORD of Hosts, the God of the armies of Israel, whom you have reviled. This day will the LORD deliver you into my hand. And I will strike you down and cut off your head. Then I will give the corpses of the Philistine camp this day to the birds of the air and to the beasts of the earth so that all the earth may know that there is a God in Israel. And then all this assembly will know that it is not by sword and spear that the LORD saves. For the battle belongs to the LORD, and He will give you into our hands. (1 Samuel 17:45–47)

The battle in our minds can change when we submit our words to the will and Word of God.

FREEDOM APPLICATION

Words produce death or life. How do you need to change your word choices? On the next page, write down some simple words you can add into your vocabulary and the words you need to remove as a reminder.

WORDS I NEED TO REMOVE	WORDS I NEED TO SPEAK

WORDS RELEASE BLESSING OR CURSE

How many things are we speaking out that contribute to the battle in our minds? How many things could we prevent from coming back on us if we would watch our words?

My husband and I have taught our children, now grown, the power of their words. We don't speak out and possess negative things over our lives as a family. If one person says something negative, another will say, "I rebuke that," or "Do you want to claim that?" We instantly take authority audibly over any negative words spoken in the atmosphere and cancel their assignment in the spiritual realm. If we say, "I'm afraid of this," we will feel fear. If we announce, "I am stressed," it reaffirms to our mind, emotions, and body that we're feeling intense pressure.

There is power in the words we speak. We can strengthen our emotions and physical body by speaking out positive proclamations over our lives, even when we aren't feeling them. I say, "Faith it till you make it." Release positive words in faith until you believe and receive the confessions you speak.

WHEN YOU SPEAK POSITIVE AFFIRMATIONS LONG ENOUGH,
YOUR SPIRIT MAN WILL ENGAGE WITH YOUR FLESH,
AND YOU WILL ARISE IN FAITH.

When you speak positive affirmations long enough, you will eventually feel them inside. Your spirit man will engage with your flesh, and you will arise in faith. Walk out your freedom by not only renewing your mind but also by watching your words. Your words are prophetically assigned and can be targeted to get a desired result. What mark do you want to hit?

PROPHETIC ACTIVATION

IDENTIFY THE BATTLE

I have to admit that I repented to my children while I wrote this chapter. It was very convicting how my parents spoke words to me that affected my actions, and it made me think of the word curses I may have spoken out over the years.

What battle do you face regarding the power of your words? How can you change? What words do you need to negate in your life?

FORGIVE AND REPENT

I never held anything against my parents because of my dad's comments or my mom's fear. I know they weren't raised the way the Lord is calling me to live. It is not their fault.

Take a moment to think about your own parents. Recognize that your parents were trained by *their* parents, so some of the things that came forth weren't their fault. Release forgiveness for any mistakes they made. Pray this prayer audibly:

Jesus, I come to You and ask for forgiveness for words that I spoke out to others that may have established a mind blockage in their lives. I pray for those people and ask You to lead them to healing and freedom. I repent of my words and forgive those who have spoken words that contributed to my mind battles. I destroy all effects of negative, hurtful, and harmful words in the natural and the spiritual.

TARGET THE BATTLE AND BREAK AGREEMENT

Declare and decree:

I break agreement and command every word that I have held on to that has affected my actions and emotions to be evicted from my mind. I disperse negative thinking and thoughts I have held on to over the years that have restrained me from movement. I no longer accept words that thwart me from being who I am called to be. I pronounce I am healed, whole, and delivered, and I disperse every attack against my mind, in Jesus's name.

RELEASE DELIVERANCE

Jesus was in the ministry of deliverance and cast out evil spirits. As you walk out your mind bondage, one of the keys to getting free and staying free is to cast out the correlating spirit that could be manifesting. It could be a spirit of lying, depression, worry, stress, anxiety, fear, mind-binding, or torment. Pray audibly and command the spirit to leave: "Spirit of _____, I cast you out, in Jesus's name."

WARFARE PRAYER DECLARATIONS

- I command all word curses to cease to activate, in Jesus's name. I bind and restrict negative words from activating.

- I confine vain imaginations from running rampant on words mentioned over my life and to me.

- I restrain memories from being vivid reminders of my past and ask the Holy Spirit to help any memories that inhibit my ability to move forward to fade away.

+ I no longer accept the negativity people said about me or word curses that were spoken over me.

+ I forcefully tear down every word that has activated negatively against me or ones I have spoken over others.

REMOVE THE BATTLE

We can't blame every battle on another person. We must take responsibility for the words we said, the feelings we took in, and the attitudes we displayed. In being set free, we need a balance between taking responsibility and putting the blame on other people.

People may have hurt you, but perhaps you could have received or perceived it differently. Ask the Holy Spirit to convict you in areas where you need to change.

PROPHETIC APPLICATION

1. What words need to be removed from the vocabulary you use to describe yourself and your situation?

2. How can you change simple statements that are facts to be released positively to activate safety, abundance, love, and grace over your life and the lives of others?

FREEDOM THOUGHT

One thought spoken out loud can change and alter the course of another person's life.

13

IDENTIFY THE BATTLE

After my husband was assigned to pastor a church, we moved away from our hometown and jumped in full force. I started a children's club, helped to organize the church, and performed office tasks. We were so excited to serve the Lord and grow a church. I helped in every way and any way I could.

Then one day, I was so weak and tired, I couldn't lift my head off of the pillow. With my head throbbing, I was unable to move. I couldn't cook, clean, or take care of the kids. I was in bed for six weeks, unable to function. I had no idea what was wrong.

After several tests, the doctors told me I had high blood pressure. Even though I didn't feel stressed, the workload I had assumed caught up to me. Once I figured out that the root cause of the hypertension was stress, I identified my battle. I began to rest, refocus, balance, and strategize how to live a ministry life without burnout. Eventually, I conquered it! Years later, I was able to get off the high blood pressure medication.

We can't conquer the battle until we identify the conflict.

I have struggled with stress, worry, and fear. Although related, each one is a different emotion and reaction. The torment and manifestation are not the same. We may intertwine such emotions, be delivered from one but not the other, or progress through them to total freedom. It is important to know our individual battles so we can bring a direct hit to our target.

> WE NEED TO REMOVE STRESS, ANXIETY, WORRY, FEAR,
> AND DEPRESSION JUST LIKE A SNIPER, HONING IN ON OUR EMOTIONAL
> AILMENTS ONE AT A TIME.

A sniper kills or demolishes his target with precision accuracy. He does not engage the entire enemy force like traditional infantry but concentrates on taking out key people or equipment. We need to remove stress, anxiety, worry, fear, and depression just like a sniper, honing in on our emotional ailments one at a time. In this manner, we can give ourselves the necessary thinking tools that apply to one particular ailment and thus overcome it effectively.

For the weapons of our warfare are not carnal, but mighty through God to the pulling down of strongholds.
(2 Corinthians 10:4)

As I have struggled with fear, stress, and worry in the past, I can clearly define the seasons in my life in which I struggled with each and received freedom. My mom was a worrier and taught me to worry about everything. I learned that most of the things we worry about never come to pass. We waste our time worrying, and it steals our peace. There are pressures in life that will occasionally stress us, but they should not consume us. When I am under pressure with a publisher's deadline, I make sure I step away, breathe, rest in the presence of the Lord, and try not to be overwhelmed with stress. Fear was my strongman. It was work to evict fear, and I had to renew my mind. There are still times it tries to capture me, but I have captured it for the most part.

One of the keys to conquering any mind ailment is rest. Rest in the presence of the Lord and renew your mind. Immediately acknowledge the attack against your thinking and train your thoughts to move away from it.

I learned about vain imaginations through Jonas Clark's book *Imaginations*.[10] If I had had that book years ago, I would not have suffered from mind bondage for so long. I could have received deliverance from my torment. However, I also must note that knowing about the different mental afflictions that we can suffer would have helped as well. For example, I wish I had known the definitions of "fear" and "torment" years ago.

DEFINING AFFLICTIONS

As we address each individual infliction by name and recognize its traits, I believe it will accelerate our freedom. I personally learned more about my situation just by looking up these definitions. For instance, I realized my struggle with fear led to torment.

WORRY

Everyone has worried at one time or another. Are you constantly worrying about something, or do you worry for a moment? The dictionary defines *worry* as "mental distress or agitation resulting from concern usually for something impending or anticipated." Depending on your level of concern, worry may not be debilitating. However, it is an area in your life where you aren't trusting God. Worrying can tire your brain when you are consistently ruminating about something. It can cause you to obsess over past events and have negative thoughts about the future.

FEAR

As we discussed in chapter five, there are many levels of fear. While our modern dictionary defines *fear* as "an unpleasant often strong emotion caused by anticipation or awareness of danger,"

10. Jonas Clark, *Imaginations: Dare to Win the Battle Against Your Mind* (Hallandale, FL: Spirit of Life Publishing, 2012).

Webster's Dictionary 1828 defines it in part as "a painful emotion or passion excited by an expectation of evil, or the apprehension of impending danger."[11] Fear is tormenting, too, because it can make you believe something bad is going to happen. Fear causes your mind to imagine circumstances and outcomes that aren't real and manifest vain imaginations.

TORMENT

Torment is mental anguish that locks you down and makes you feel as if your mind is paralyzed. It is *debilitating*, defined by *Merriam-Webster* as "causing serious impairment of strength or ability to function." Torment attacks you and ties you up mentally, emotionally, and spiritually, hindering your ability to pray and worship to fight the battle.

STRESS

My personal definition of *stress* is mental pressure or tension. Stress can affect our body physically or mentally; it's a feeling of being overwhelmed, pressured, and fatigued. A person or a situation can cause stress in our life, and the feeling can last for a certain season or reason.

ANXIETY

Anxiety affects your mind and body. *Webster's Dictionary 1828* defines it as concern "respecting some event, future or uncertain, which disturbs the mind, and keeps it in a state of painful uneasiness. It expresses more than uneasiness or disturbance, and even more than trouble...It usually springs from fear or serious apprehension of evil, and involves a suspense respecting an event, and often, a perplexity of mind, to know how to shape our conduct."[12]

---

11. webstersdictionary1828.com/Dictionary/fear.
12. webstersdictionary1828.com/Dictionary/anxiety.

> ANXIETY CAN MAKE YOU FEEL ON EDGE,
> LIKE SOMETHING IS ABOUT TO HAPPEN. IT MAY BE ACCOMPANIED BY
> PANIC OR A SUDDEN, OVERPOWERING FRIGHT.

Anxiety can make you feel on edge, like something is about to happen. Your heart can race, or you can feel as if something will occur or scare you at any moment. Your heart can rapidly beat through your chest, or you can feel uncomfortable and uneasy. It may be accompanied by panic or a sudden, overpowering fright.

DEPRESSION

Depression is a deep sadness. *Merriam-Webster* defines it as "a mood disorder that is marked by varying degrees of sadness, despair, and loneliness and that is typically accompanied by inactivity, guilt, loss of concentration, social withdrawal, sleep disturbances, and sometimes suicidal tendencies."

People can experience different types of depression, such as:

+ Postpartum. This is the stress, anxiety, worry, and tiredness that can occur following the delivery of a baby.

+ Seasonal affective disorder. This depression is associated with a lack of natural light, particularly during winter months.

+ Situational. A stressful or traumatic event can cause short-term depression.

+ Major depression. This is persistent sadness that affects how you think, feel, and act.

FREEDOM APPLICATION

We all have an area in which we struggle, but freedom is available. Use the following chart to categorize your feelings. Circle all of the feelings that manifest in your life and write your identifying thoughts underneath. Can you identify the greatest source of your battle?

FEAR	STRESS	ANXIETY	DEPRESSION	WORRY

FREEDOM APPLICATION

1. What emotional condition do you feel you have had over the years? How do you think you are suffering?

_____

_____

2. Using the descriptions you've provided, what mental struggle would you categorize as evident in yourself?

_____

_____

3. Do your answers to these two questions differ?

_____

_____

I have struggled with fear for years. I also know I have struggled with worry and stress during some portions of my life. While doing research for this book, I discovered that I don't suffer the mental fatigue of stress except when I am under intense deadlines. I did worry, but worry is not same as fear.

The definitions I have provided and the descriptions I've asked you to write are not meant to be detrimental. I don't want you to fall into a place of condemnation by discovering how much you struggle. Instead, I want to help you determine where your struggles are, and where you have obtained victory. You may think you have not made any progress, but every little victory is a step in the right direction.

When dealing with demonic strongholds and casting out demons, we must be able to identify the exact demon and call it out by name. Personally, I was probably plagued with torment more than fear as I looked at those definitions. I must mention, however, that every emotional ailment is torment.

Whether your mind is bound and you can't pull it back into a positive direction, or demonic spirits are causing you fear, depression, or anxiety, it is all torment. I want to encourage you to go back and look at the definitions again and then compare them with your manifestations. Let's do this exercise differently this time.

FREEDOM APPLICATION

1. I have been manifesting these feelings or emotions:

_____

_____

2. It feels like this when it happens:

_____

_____

3. I have experienced the following kind of torment:

_____

_____

Now that you have done these exercises, what truth have you discovered? Have you received freedom, clarity, or understanding by just being able to identify your mind battle? Is there freedom that has manifested forth, or do you see yourself gaining victory in some areas?

WELLNESS DEFINED

There are different types of wellness to describe the soul part of us, which is our mind, will, and emotions. Defining these types can assist us in identifying our mind struggles so that we can heal. The types of wellness affecting our souls include:

+ Emotional health – our feelings, both positive and negative.

+ Mental health – our thinking, behavior, and feeling. For this exercise, we are going to concentrate on the thinking aspect.

+ Spiritual health – our spirit man and spiritual walk in relationship to the Lord Jesus.

+ Social health – relating, interacting, and forming relationships, and how we adapt to social settings.

+ Intellectual health – our creative potential and desire to increase understanding and be open to new ideas.

We want to define wellness because most mind battles involve an interconnected struggle. Wellness triggers that can lead to mind battles include unworthiness, unfairness, emotional abuse, being controlled, hurt, and condemnation. There is always a root cause for our emotions, something greater or deeper that we need to seek, locate, and identify. It is like searching for a treasure chest inside the depths of the soul. On the outside, the chest may be rusty, dirty, or covered with debris, but when you open it up, you discover beautiful jewels that represent you—diamonds, emeralds, sapphires, and rubies. The outside of our souls may be covered with areas that we need to clean up, chip off, and remove, but there's a treasure waiting for us inside.

> THE OUTSIDE OF OUR SOULS MAY BE COVERED WITH AREAS
> THAT WE NEED TO CLEAN UP, CHIP OFF,
> AND REMOVE, BUT THERE'S A TREASURE WAITING FOR US INSIDE.

Looking over the definitions of wellness, which ones can you relate to as part of your struggle? Categorize your emotions and feelings. Can you decipher where you need to set a wellness goal?

As we discussed in chapter two, we may process and analyze when we are pondering our mind battles. However, we need to discern whether the battle is mental or emotional. Ask yourself:

+ Is my issue mental, a thinking problem, in that I can feel this affecting my thinking, or I can't wrap my mind around this concept?

+ Is my issue emotional, a feeling that arises within me and causes an adverse reaction such as sadness, tears, feelings of inadequacy, or fear?

We want to target your battle as accurately as a sniper. As we identify the specific problem, we can move forward in a vast way to get maximum impact in your battle.

FREEDOM APPLICATION

1. Areas of mental battles in which I need freedom.

2. Areas of emotional battles in which I need freedom.

No one can tell you what your battle is or how you struggle with it. Even though both of us may have struggled with fear, we process, analyze, feel, and think in different ways. No one can directly relate to your issue except you.

For example, my friend and I were pregnant at the same time, and both of us miscarried. I cried and grieved, but I made it through it with the help of the Lord and my family. My friend had to seek counseling. We had a similar experience, but processed it differently and took different paths to heal.

This is one reason why I always lead people to seek the Holy Spirit. He is the only one who knows what you experienced, how you felt, and how it is still affecting you. My prayer is that you have used this book as a means to cooperate and depend on the Holy Spirit for your complete healing.

Jesus is *Jehovah Rapha*, our Healer. The Holy Spirit convicts, teaches, and guides us as our friend who leads us to Jesus. May your utter dependence be upon Him as you seek your healing.

PROPHETIC ACTIVATION

IDENTIFY THE BATTLE

Struggles with emotional battles are common, so when you experience one, it should not bring forth shame or condemnation. Expose your battle and expose the enemy. As you identify your battle, reach out to someone you trust for accountability. Ask them to pray for you and occasionally check in on you during your deliverance process. You *can* be free. Identifying the way you feel will be the best step to receive your freedom.

FORGIVE AND REPENT

Shame, condemnation, regret, and insecurity can attack your mind. You may take a lot of those feelings in and harbor them. Even though you may have had some responsibility, your battle is truly not your fault. Forgiving yourself can be the hardest part of the battle.

Pray audibly this prayer of forgiveness:

Jesus, forgive me if I did anything to contribute to the battle. I take a step today to forgive myself. I release myself from guilt, shame, and condemnation. I forgive myself. I forgive myself. I forgive myself. Thank You, Jesus, for Your forgiveness and the freedom You have purchased for me.

TARGET THE BATTLE AND BREAK AGREEMENT

Speak out and decree:

I break agreement and say that I am not a victim. I am victorious. I am everything God's Word says I can be, and the will of God manifests in my life. I release doubt and unbelief that I can change and be different. I raise my expectations for prosperous thinking and an attitude of gratitude. Help me, Holy Spirit. Walk with me every day to live my new life of freedom.

WARFARE PRAYER DECLARATIONS

+ I decree that I am obtaining my mind freedom, in Jesus's name. The good things of God are coming my way!

+ I proclaim that whom the Son sets free is free indeed! I am receiving my freedom!

+ I command every good and God thought to come forth in my life. My mind thinks good thoughts!

+ I speak and pronounce that my transformation is here. I'm receiving impartation and activation.

+ I call forth the love of God to wash over every mind ailment and heal me with His love.

RELEASE DELIVERANCE

Jesus was in the ministry of deliverance and cast out evil spirits. As you walk out your mind bondage, one of the keys to getting free and staying free is to cast out the correlating spirit that could be manifesting. It could be a spirit of lying, depression, worry, stress, anxiety, fear, mind-binding, or torment. Pray audibly and command the spirit to leave: "Spirit of _____, I cast you out, in Jesus's name."

REMOVE THE BATTLE

Receiving freedom takes time and commitment. You may have tried to press through to your breakthrough before, but it didn't seem to work out. How can you commit to making this time be different? How can you keep persevering and not give up? What plan can you develop and who can hold you accountable so that you break free and stay free?

PROPHETIC APPLICATION

1. Identify where you may be blaming yourself for your problems.

2. Develop a plan to assist someone you love to freedom. Buy them a copy of this book so they can work through it and break free of their mind battles.

FREEDOM THOUGHT

You can change. It is not beyond you. Seek the Holy Spirit and believe in God's promises for you.

CLOSING PROPHETIC WORD

Now you are entering into a new season. A season you have never experienced before. It's okay if you don't know what it looks like. Don't try to figure it out. You may not recognize something about yourself and how your mind thinks, but it is all good. I, God, am right here with you. I will get you through it. I will lead you through it. Listen to My still, small voice. You do hear from Me. Focus and hone in and listen to Me. When fear tries to arise, listen to Me, listen to My direction, and use the tools in this book as your instruction. You are on a new journey, an unfamiliar journey, but a journey that is going to be great. I am getting ready to do a new thing. Ride the waves of refreshing this new thing, this new mind renewal, will bring. I'm getting ready to storm the gates of hell on your behalf. Trust Me for this new thing. I will release and accomplish in your life. I love you, My child. Now go and live your life to the fullest and release peace.

ABOUT THE AUTHOR

Kathy DeGraw is a prophetic deliverance minister releasing the love and power of God. She loves to ignite and activate people, release prophetic destinies, and deliver people from the bondage of the enemy. In her meetings, the glory of God appears, and people are supernaturally healed and delivered as the Word of God goes forth and is preached.

Kathy is the founder of Kathy DeGraw Ministries and K Advancement LLC. She enjoys ministering and releasing the love and fire of the Holy Spirit, teaching believers how to walk in the fullness of God and release their prophetic potential. She uses her prophetic anointing to deliver people from the powers of darkness and goes deep in the ministry of deliverance to eradicate strongholds, expose the root causes and legal rights of the enemy, and evict evil principalities.

Kathy hosts a weekly podcast show called *Prophetic Spiritual Warfare* that has reached more than one million listeners. She has been a guest on *The Jim Bakker Show* and *Sid Roth's It's Supernatural!* Kathy is a prophetic voice and writer on *The Elijah List, Charisma Magazine, Prophecy Investigators,* and *Spirit Fuel.* She has a clear and unique gift of discernment and operates in a strong prophetic, healing, and deliverance anointing. In addition to *Mind Battles,* she has published several books, including *Prophetic Spiritual Warfare,* based on her podcast.

Kathy is married to her best friend, Pastor Ron DeGraw. They reside in Michigan and are the parents of three adult children.

Keep in touch with Kathy at:

www.kathydegrawministries.org

admin@degrawministries.org

www.facebook.com/kathydegraw

www.youtube.com/c/KathyDeGraw

Welcome to Our House!

We Have a Special Gift for You

It is our privilege and pleasure to share in your love of Christian books. We are committed to bringing you authors and books that feed, challenge, and enrich your faith.

To show our appreciation, we invite you to sign up to receive a specially selected **Reader Appreciation Gift**, with our compliments. Just go to the Web address at the bottom of this page.

God bless you as you seek a deeper walk with Him!

WE HAVE A GIFT FOR YOU. VISIT:

whpub.me/nonfictionthx

WHITAKER
HOUSE